Pelican Books

Understanding and Helping the Schizophrenic
A Guide for Family and Friends

Silvano Arieti, M.D., a noted psychiatrist and psychoanalyst, is
Professor of Clinical Psychiatry at New York Medical College and
editor-in-chief of the monumental, six-volume *American Handbook
of Psychiatry*. Among his many honours Dr Arieti has received the
Frieda Fromm-Reichmann Award for his contribution to
the knowledge and understanding of schizophrenia and the Emil
A Gutheil Medal for outstanding contributions to psychiatry and
psychotherapy.

Justin Schlicht, M.B., B.S., M.Sc., M.R.C.Psych., L.R.C.P.,
M.R.C.S., is Consultant Psychotherapist to the Bethlem Royal
Hospital and the Maudsley Hospital.

Silvano Arieti

Understanding and Helping the Schizophrenic

A Guide for Family and Friends

British edition revised and adapted by Dr Justin Schlicht

Penguin Books

Penguin Books Ltd, Harmondsworth, Middlesex, England
Viking Penguin Inc., 40 West 23rd Street, New York, New York 10010, U.S.A.
Penguin Books Australia Ltd, Ringwood, Victoria, Australia
Penguin Books Canada Ltd, 2801 John Street, Markham, Ontario, Canada L3R 1B4
Penguin Books (N.Z.) Ltd, 182–190 Wairau Road, Auckland 10, New Zealand

First published in the U.S.A. by Basic Books 1979
This edition first published in Pelican Books 1981
Reprinted 1984

Printed and bound in Great Britain by
Cox & Wyman Ltd, Reading
Filmset in Itek Times New Roman

Contents

Preface

The first aim of this book is to explain to the general reader what is known and what remains to be known about schizophrenia, a psychiatric condition that afflicts more than three million Americans and more than forty million persons around the world. I hope to explain the patient's unreal world, the various dimensions of his predicament, the development of his particular type of personality, his confrontation with his individual psychological problems, and his possible return to health.

The amazing lack of knowledge in this field permits the old inaccuracies and misconceptions to remain, the fears to grow (often beyond proportion), the prejudices to persist, and the offers of help to be denied or only hesitantly and half-heartedly made. I want to show that even before he recovers, the schizophrenic is much closer to us than to the mentally ill character of the television show or the deranged relative in literature. He may be our next-door neighbor rather than a stranger.

But this first aim only prepares for the book's second and main purpose: indicating to the family, friends, and anyone concerned how to participate in the task of helping the patient to regain his health or to greatly improve. It is important to learn what to do first, what treatments are available and how to obtain them, what hospitalization can offer, and most of all how to live with the patient day by day, how to talk to him, what arrangements to make for him.

For many years the role of the family in the causation of schizophrenia was seen from a particular, probably biased, stance, and the participation of the family in the reintegration and rehabilitation of the patient was viewed with skepticism. In this book I seek to promote a different climate, one in keeping with recent findings. Fortunately the family is not alone. As this book will indicate, psychiatrists, other professionals, paraprofessionals, hospitals, halfway houses, and many other people and institutions are there, ready to participate in the great enterprise, and most of the time they do excellent work. But with the number of patients who remain a serious problem, we may borrow an expression used by President Truman in a different context: the buck stops there, in the family. There is no other or better place to turn, no place where enlightenment and guidance are more needed and more appreciated.

A third aim of this book is to outline the pioneer efforts we can make to prevent disorders and finally to show how even a pathological mental condition can reveal notions useful to other aspects of life.

This, of course, is not a book that covers the whole vast field. Many topics of no direct interest to the general reader have been left out. Those who want a deeper discussion of the issues, or an exposition of related issues, may find them in my book *Interpretation of Schizophrenia*, or in the many other books on this subject. All major points of view and forms of treatment have been reported in this book. However, the reader will recognize what views I share or to what I attribute more importance. To have forced myself to take a completely objective position toward all possible interpretations and treatments would have required a detachment antithetical to my approach to schizophrenia.

Some readers will observe that for many questions no definite answer is given. To them I must reply that schizophrenia is not like mumps or measles. The limitation of our knowledge about a condition that involves all the aspects of human existence is to a large extent due to the fact that there is no end to the mystery of life. But if the journey is endless, so is our possibility for understanding, growing, and improving.

I do not consider myself the only author of this book. Not only must I acknowledge that I have learned much from the work of a large number of colleagues, but I must also add that I consider my

many patients, who through the years have given me their
confidence and trust, as my coauthors. To them go my thanks.
With them I maintain the friendship and comradeship that derive
from the sharing of ideas, feelings, innovations, surprises, and
hopes.

SILVANO ARIETI

1. We Cannot Ignore Schizophrenia

7 A.M. The alarm clock wakes Joseph Monrot. It continues to ring and ring, louder and louder, and seems never to stop. Joseph gets up. The ringing is now almost deafening. He covers his ears, but he still hears it. He does not know what to make of this. He goes to the window and opens it, and the loud noise of the alarm clock spreads through the air, presumably heard by everybody. At first it sounds like the siren of a police car, then of a fire engine; finally it seems so powerful as to transmit a warning signal to the whole city. The streets, too, are unusual this morning. The buildings have assumed funny shapes. Everything is brightly hued, like Technicolor. In the twenty-four years of his young life Joseph Monrot has never experienced a similar sense of foreboding and of ominous mystery.

It is dusk, and Ann Marie Rufell is heading for home, just a few blocks away. But the dusk is darker than at the beginning of other evenings, and the lights that are coming on are dimmer than usual. The noises of the city are different – continuous, with an incessant sound of dismay, sometimes fading away and then coming back, like waves. There is a whispering in the air, diffused, unintelligible. Gradually, words become clearly distinguishable. They are about her. She looks backward, and there they are, peculiar men with grotesque faces who follow her. What do they want from a poor, innocent, twenty-two-year-old girl? They are spying on her. They may want to catch up with her and perhaps kidnap her. She runs home in a state of panic, panting. Her trembling hands try to find the keyhole; she opens the door, bursts into tears, and screams, 'Mother, Mother, they're following me, they're after me!'

Joseph Monrot and Ann Marie Rufell are having acute attacks of schizophrenia.

If Joseph or Ann Marie is a member of your family, his or her suffering immediately becomes your suffering, and his or her problem your most crucial problem. You will want to learn all you can about this strange illness so that you can try to understand what the person is experiencing and how to cope with the situation, and possibly to go beyond coping to helping. You will want to know what causes the disease and what can be done to cure it.

If a family member was recently discharged from a hospital, you will want to know how to live with him day by day, how to recognize the signs of an impending new schizophrenic episode, what kinds of emergencies might arise, and how to handle them if they do. If you are fortunate enough never to have had the disease touch your family, you may have a friend or a neighbor who has suffered from it, and you may want to know how much progress in understanding the disease has been made in recent years and how much is still in need of being clarified.

Even if you do not know anyone who has been struck by this illness, you may have encountered patients who have been discharged and are now in the community. You may be motivated to increase your knowledge of this condition because of your concern for those fellow human beings who are afflicted by it. You may want to know how to overcome prejudices about them as they are reintegrated into society, even more so when you see some of the most pitiful cases wandering the streets as hobos or derelicts. As a matter of fact, in recent years psychiatric patients, mostly schizophrenics, have been discharged from public hospitals in large numbers. (In one year alone in New York State 50,000 psychiatric patients were discharged.) This policy of discharge has also been vigorously pursued in the United Kingdom.

You may also have heard or read something about schizophrenia and gathered enough information to conclude that to know about schizophrenia means to know a great deal about the human condition and predicament.

Finally, and most crucially, if the person who has suffered or is still suffering from schizophrenia is you, you may want to know how the patient recovers in many cases and improves in many others, and how, in many instances, although the illness may limit some functions, it can add new dimensions to life.

All these issues, many of them previously ignored, will be discussed in the pages that follow.

Schizophrenia cannot be ignored. In recent years, however, much more attention has been paid to other diseases. Coronary disease, cancer, diabetes – these have captured the public interest. Numerous campaigns have been devised to combat these illnesses and have received immediate support from the public. Schizophrenia has not stimulated equal concern. And yet, in spite of the discharge of numerous schizophrenics from hospitals, more hospital beds are still occupied by schizophrenics than by people suffering from any other disease. No other condition creates such heavy economic burdens for the state or the family. A few years ago the annual cost of schizophrenia to the nation was estimated at $14 billion; today it is probably more than twice that amount. Few conditions handicap people for such a length of time. Although it is true that schizophrenia can be of very short duration – twenty-four- or forty-eight-hour schizophrenia has been described – it is also true that there are some cases, fortunately in rapidly decreasing numbers, in which the illness starts at the time of puberty or shortly thereafter and lasts for the entire life of the patient, who may live into his nineties.

Even if we compare public concern over schizophrenia with that caused by other psychiatric conditions only, we can easily affirm that several other psychiatric disorders – among them alcoholism, drug addiction, and depression – have recently received more attention from the public at large and from the press. If we assess the gravity of an illness solely by the number of people who are affected by it, then alcoholism deserves the greatest attention. But if we evaluate importance in terms of the severity of mental disturbance, or of the degree of interference with the functions of mental health, then we must conclude that no other problem is of greater magnitude than schizophrenia.

When we consider the impact of schizophrenia on the present generation (there are about 40 million schizophrenics in the world), we can conclude that no war in history has produced so many victims, wounded so many people. No earthquake has exacted so high a toll; no other condition that we know of has deprived so many young people of the promise of life.

Why, then, has schizophrenia received relatively little attention in the press and other media directed at the general public? There is no single answer, but we can enumerate a combination of factors that have reinforced each other. Many people, discouraged by the numerous problems that schizophrenia presents, assume an attitude of denial; that is, they act as if schizophrenia does not exist, or as if they feel the best way to deal with it is to ignore it.

Some people – unfortunately among them even a few professionals – insist that schizophrenia does not exist, that it is a myth, and they succeed in getting considerable attention from the public and from the press because of the sensational nature of their statements. Some of these people who deny the existence of schizophrenia or who refuse to consider it an illness are well intentioned. They remain impervious to the presence of this serious mental condition either because they cannot believe that an illness can exist without visible body changes or because they refuse to accept the concept now firmly established (especially since Freud), that many psychiatric illnesses are psychosomatic, that is, the result at least in part of emotional factors. They refuse to recognize the revolution that occurred in medicine when it became established that not every illness presupposes an abnormal anatomical transformation of some cells of the body. Although this concept, which was originally formulated by the German pathologist Virchow, is valid for the majority of illnesses, it is not in others, such as those in which an alteration of cells occurs only *after* an emotional disorder. In still other diseases the alteration may occur not in the anatomical *structure* of the cells but in the way some cells *function*. The disease is then called *functional*. In a functional disease the biochemistry may be altered and become abnormal to a considerable degree, even though the basic anatomical structure is unchanged.

Others deny the existence of schizophrenia on the grounds that this mental condition cannot be defined, so different are its manifestations from those of other diseases and so debatable its causes. But to be able to define anything exactly means to know that thing perfectly. If we had waited, for example, to define electricity or the atom until we knew everything there is to know about them, science would have made no progress. Even now, as a matter of fact, many people can argue that we do not know what electricity is, although we know many of its characteristics and the laws by which electrical energy is regulated. The word *atom*, in Greek, means something that cannot be further divided. This is a completely inaccurate definition of an atom, yet without such working definitions physical chemistry would not have advanced.

When the subject is schizophrenia, there is much we already know. Libraries have been filled with books about this disorder, and the successes we achieve today in treating this condition would certainly shock Emil Kraepelin, the first psychiatrist to describe schizophrenia, which he called *dementia praecox*. When he wrote his major book in 1896, Kraepelin believed that every case of schizophrenia was ineluctably destined to progressively decline, with no possibility of recovery or improvement. Fortunately, that belief is no longer current.

If we scratch the surface and search for unconscious reasons for denying the existence of what is obvious and greatly disturbing, we eventually come to recognize that this denial is founded on a common and ancient prejudice toward mental illnesses – so-called madness, craziness, or insanity – of which schizophrenia is the most typical representative. The fear of mental illness, or the concept of mental illness as something to be ashamed of or horrified by, leads to its denial. The belief that we, too, if we are eccentric or if we assume an extremist, controversial, or unpopular position, may be wrongly labeled as schizophrenics, leads to its denial. The apprehension that we may be secretly suffering from this disorder, leads to its denial. The absurd fear that we may be *the direct and only cause* of schizophrenia in others, especially our children, and that we may have to face the resultant guilt, leads to its denial. The absolutely unfounded belief that nothing can be done about it also leads to its denial. In fact, however, approximately one out of three patients recovers completely, and more than one-third improve sufficiently to live adequate lives.

It is worth mentioning that the prejudice towards mental illness is rapidly diminishing and is much less pronounced than it used to be; however, it still exists, especially among certain social classes and in some geographical areas. This prejudice is manifested when mental illness is called a *stigma*, that is, a discrediting characteristic. The burden was greater in the past when schizophrenics were considered more prone to violence and to aggressive antisocial behavior, a conception that has proved wrong. Violent actions are no more frequent among schizophrenics than among the general population. However, certain characteristics of the schizophrenic are among those that any society dislikes. The schizophrenic does not always behave in a way that is considered appropriate to the circumstances or in accordance with the expectations of society. Society trusts order, solidarity, and conformity to its own mores. As the great sociologist Emile Durkheim stated, any discriminatory attitude toward the deviant is intended to reassure the members of the society who want to preserve its stability and prevent threats to it. The schizophrenic is likely to sleep during the day and be up at night; to dress inappropriately on many occasions, such as going to a funeral in blue jeans; and to look away when spoken to. However, persons who have studied and observed the schizophrenic know that his nonconformance is not a threat to others' conformity but is a private affair. The patient does not seek proselytes; he does not want to be a reformer. What could be considered inappropriateness, bizarreness, indifference, or apathy is not tinged with evil but is rather an expression of deviance.

The general public is gradually learning that the deviance of the schizophrenic is not socially dangerous. Nevertheless, the fact remains that because he is different, the patient appears to be a stranger among his own people, a person with whom it is difficult to identify. When we think of the alcoholic or the depressed person, the identification is easier to make. Most of us like to drink occasionally, and all of us have been depressed at some time in our lives.

The schizophrenic is viewed scornfully because, when he is withdrawn, he gives the impression of either being afraid of the world or rejecting the world. At times he seems to assume the pose that he has nothing to do with his environment or that he views the entire universe with boundless disdain. As I shall show later, this is far from the truth. It is only the impression the schizophrenic conveys to others, and often to himself as well. His secret wish is to rejoin the human community. When the paranoid schizophrenic acts as a collector of alleged injustices or finds fault with everybody, he does so only with his overt actions and his superficial layers of thinking. His illness has made him devise these attitudes as a protection against the feeling of distrust that pervades him.

Schizophrenia is not something that we need to feel ashamed of or guilty about, just as we are not ashamed of or guilty for earthquakes that may occur where we live. And unlike earthquakes, schizophrenia is a phenomenon that we can do a great deal about. If there is something we should feel ashamed of or guilty for, it is our denial of the problem, our doing nothing to combat the disorder or to prevent it. Even if schizophrenia is partially or indirectly related to some unfavorable or unfair conditions of our society, we must not just feel ashamed or neglectful but must try to identify and alleviate these conditions. In the fact that schizophrenia is still with us we must find an additional incentive to improve the ways in which we organize our environment and our social institutions, live within our families, and affect one another.

I have so far considered the collective impact of schizophrenia, but the most tragic drama of this mental disorder unfolds in the individual sufferer.

Schizophrenia generally does not cause physical pain, but the mental agony that it engenders may become so great that the patient would gladly trade it for physical pain. Some patients inflict physical injuries on themselves, hoping that the pain will cancel out the mental anguish. This anguish, which is particularly pronounced in the initial stage of the illness, is in its turn preceded by a longer unseen, uncared-for, and often unsuspected suffering that may go back to early childhood. During the initial stage and afterward, the patient often goes through the horror of seeing himself no longer in communication with the world. He does not understand others, and others no longer understand him. He feels lonely and isolated and yet not isolated enough, because he is convinced that obscure surrounding forces, undefinable evils, or specific people are after him to do him harm. Unless he recovers or improves – and let me repeat that the odds are two to one in his favour that he will – a progressive decline of his functions is likely to occur. He will become less and less capable of enjoying life, of receiving and giving, of hoping and creating. Time does not march on for him any more. It cannot go forward, just as it cannot go backward. It is arrested at the present state of vast devastation.

It is important to have compassion for the mentally ill, to understand their suffering, and to overcome prejudices toward them, but it is even more important for us to develop a sense of kinship for the patient, because it implies compassion and abolition of prejudice. If we do, the likelihood of our being able to help will also increase. In many cases we may even admire the patient.

If I seem to be making curious claims, it is not because I think the schizophrenic knows the supreme truth, or a higher truth concealed from the rest of us. This is an extremist position taken by Ronald Laing, a British psychiatrist who has achieved much more popularity among the lay public than within the psychiatric profession. No human being knows the supreme truth, certainly not the schizophrenic, who is unable most of the time to distinguish reality from fantasy. Rather, I believe we may admire the schizophrenic because he is a person who takes the world seriously, and because he cannot accept what he finds unacceptable in life. However, he cannot cope with the situation and comes to feel that he is both unaccepted and unacceptable. He does not want to capitulate to what he considers a bad environment, but he feels he has no strength to put up an efficient protest.

Why must we feel kinship with him? Because there is at least a speck of deviance in each of us, but unlike the schizophrenic, we are afraid to show it. He inflates his deviance; we bury ours whenever possible. We, too, feel rejected at times or, conversely, feel prone to reject, ready to blame or feel blamed. Not infrequently we are partners of the schizophrenic in his protest, but we remain silent.

The schizophrenic may scream, but his scream has a sound of sickness and his protestation takes strange forms, like Joseph Monrot's protest, which became the ring of the alarm clock that deafened the whole city, or Ann Marie Rufell's protest, which became a reaction of horror at the sight of grotesque men who pursued her and wanted to do her harm.

In coming to understand the schizophrenic the reader will discover not only aspects of human horror and tragedy, but also the strength, the versatility, and the richness of the human mind. How is it possible to do so in studying an illness? The study of schizophrenia takes us into the realm of the irrational, but the irrational is also human and has a 'rationality' and richness of its own. What is more irrational than a dream? Certainly we cannot take literally a dream that makes us live at once in different times, confuse locations, misidentify people, or do things that we would never do when we are awake. And yet Freud's great discovery about the meaning of dreams disclosed the rational work the mind performs when it dreams. What Freud revealed to us about dreams has enabled us to understand new dimensions of the human spirit. Similarly, when we study schizophrenia, we explore a world of imagination, a world where that which gains supremacy is not reality, but a metaphor or a universe made of metaphors. Whereas so-called normal persons remain prisoners of reality, the schizophrenic becomes a fugitive from it. While we remain firmly earthbound, he is like an astronaut who intends to explore better worlds; but unlike real astronauts, the schizophrenic has serious difficulties in returning to our humble planet. His attempt to escape from humanity is futile because he will always be human. It is because he is so human and so involved with this world that he becomes schizophrenic. In this book we shall develop an understanding of how this happens. We shall also accompany the patient into the mysterious yet human worlds of his imagination.

In another book, *Creativity: The Magic Synthesis*, I have shown that the schizophrenic is not the only fugitive from reality. The creative person, too, feels a prisoner in the midst of things as they really are and wants to change them by adding something that will make the world more beautiful, more understandable, or more controllable. As I have demonstrated, scientists, poets, artists, playwrights, and other creative people use some mental processes similar to those used by the schizophrenic – and by the normal person when he dreams. Creative people are able to fuse these strange mental processes with the usual logical mechanisms of the mind, and the result is creative work and creative products. The schizophrenic cannot make this laborious synthesis. He uses imaginative processes in destructive ways. Nevertheless, as I have shown in that earlier book, the study of these mechanisms clarifies to a considerable extent the complexity of a creative person. Schizophrenia thus does not remain just a medical and humane concern. It is true that our consideration, commitment, and involvement derive from our great concern for people who suffer from this condition. But in addition, the study of this disorder will give us the possibility of seeing from unusual perspectives the labyrinth of the human mind – that ever-unfolding and never-finished entity that has no equal for complexity in the world known to science. By studying schizophrenia we examine in a unique way the great enigma of the human being, his eternal wavering between truth and illusion; his constant uncertainty between love and hate; his conflict between his desire to embrace his fellow men and his fear of them; and his circuitous journey between increasing suspiciousness and absolute faith, between his insatiable hunger for other people and his deep, interminable isolation and loneliness. These extremes encompass the vast panorama of human existence.

Again and again in this chapter I have referred to a condition that I have not defined. What is schizophrenia? Schizophrenia is not so easy to define as is pneumonia, mumps, or even depression. I shall offer more accurate definitions, in accordance with the knowledge added by other chapters, but for the time being we shall call schizophrenia an abnormal condition of the mind that affects only human beings; drastically changes their modes of thinking, feeling, and dealing with the world; *makes them confuse fantasy with reality;* and leads them to maladaptive ways of living.

2. Warnings of Schizophrenia to Come

When Warnings Are Ignored

Joseph Monrot and Ann Marie Rufell, whom I mentioned at the beginning of Chapter 1, suddenly became acutely ill, and everybody who knew them was utterly shocked. These two young people seemed to do so well in life and appeared so well-adjusted. Did their schizophrenia come from the blue, like lightning and thunder from a clear and shining sky?

Schizophrenia at times comes unexpectedly, at other times after a small occurrence, like a minor accident, that the average person would be able to master or endure without unusual distress. Is it really true that there are no warnings of schizophrenia to come? Let us examine several cases that offer different possibilities. Although schizophrenia can come at any age, in this chapter we shall concentrate on its occurrence in young adulthood (eighteen to twenty-four years of age), the most susceptible period. First, I want to stress that all cases described in this book are authentic and are reported as they really occurred, including those of Joseph Monrot and Ann Marie Rufell. Only the names given to the patients are fictitious.

I remember a patient whom I examined some years ago, not too long after the end of World War II. He had been in a minor accident while driving a bus, having been hired as a driver only two days before. The accident amounted to very little: the bus collided with a car, which sustained minimal damage. Nobody was hurt. The patient had nevertheless become agitated and had to return home. His wife immediately brought him to my office.

She told me that the accident had taken place seven hours before, and since then her husband had talked nonsense. According to her, the man had shown no abnormality whatever prior to the accident She was pregnant, and the night before they had talked about their future plans and about the expected baby, and they were very happy. When I saw the patient, he was excited and could not stay still. He recognized that something important was disturbing him, but he was not able to say what it was. During the consultation my phone rang twice. Each time he thought that someone was calling me concerning him. They must be after him. They must know where he is. Because he heard the voice of a woman at the end of the line, he assumed that it was the voice of his aunt. She was talking to me about him. He did not know what was happening. Everything was in motion, confused and strange.

Following are some of his statements, which I took down verbatim. 'The world is going very fast; it keeps spinning on an axe [sic] but keeps going. If the people of the world are going a little faster, they try to go with the world, and they shouldn't. It is my desperate opinion that the people are rushing slowly and slowly and when they reach a certain point, they start to realize that they are going fast or slow, and they cannot be judges of the world as it is spinning. The world has changed, is going fast, keeps going, going. I couldn't keep up with it.'

After I completed the examination, I recommended immediate hospitalization, and the patient recovered in a few months. Is it true that he had not shown any sign of trouble before the accident?

As a matter of fact, the patient had come to see me before, shortly after his return from the war. He had had difficulty readjusting to civilian life then and had been uncertain as to whether or not he should reenlist in the army. He had come to see me at the suggestion of the Veterans Administration Office of Rehabilitation. The patient was then engaged to be married but was unemployed. At the end of the second session he felt that he did not want any more treatment, and I was not able to persuade him to continue. I tried to explain to him that he appeared very anxious, and that, although some apprehension was justified because he was unemployed and yet wanted to get married, his anxiety was excessive. I suggested that he and I try to discover why he was so insecure and to see what we could do about it. He did not agree with me, especially since his family had strongly reinforced his belief that there was nothing wrong with him, that his only difficulty was lack of an occupation, and that once he found a job every difficulty in his life would be solved.

Although he stressed the role his family had played in convincing him, he forbade me to communicate with them. One of the reasons he gave for discontinuing treatment was that he had to go out of town to visit wealthy and prominent relatives who probably would offer him a good position. There was no sign of schizophrenia when I saw this patient: nevertheless I knew that his condition was precarious.

Three months later I received the telephone call from his wife. Upon arriving at my office she added that she and the patient had been married only one month. His relatives had not kept their promise, but the patient had had several odd jobs, and 'everything seemed to be all right.' Two days before, he had secured the position as bus driver.

I believe we are in a position to evaluate what is behind this 'surprising' attack of schizophrenia. After returning from the army, the patient had made an attempt to adjust to civilian life. But old personal difficulties, like his shyness, fearfulness, indecision, and lack of initiative – which were not obvious as long as he was in the army – surfaced again once he became a civilian, and they hindered his readjustment. At the same time that his personal difficulties returned, the demands he felt were made on him, or that he made on himself, put him in a state of unrest. He felt that as soon as possible he should marry the girl to whom he had been engaged for so long and who had waited for his return. His relatives disappointed him, and his dependence on them proved a mistake. Of course, he should not have depended on them, but on his own resources. However, he did not trust himself; he was insecure, especially because he had no special skills to offer any prospective employer. He had not learned a profession or a trade because a deep-seated feeling of inferiority had made him believe that he would not do well in any school. Even now his feeling of insecurity prevented him from pursuing an education under the G.I. Bill of Rights. A series of unusual and unpleasant circumstances in his childhood had determined this feeling of inadequacy.

In spite of all this, the patient had finally secured a good job as a bus driver; two days later he had the accident. He believed he would lose the job, and this belief reinforced his deep feeling of worthlessness. The accident was, to him, proof of his inherent incompetence, especially since he attached so much importance to having a job. Almost all his security was precariously founded on his having a gainful position. Now nobody would have any confidence in him. His relatives were right in not trusting him with a job. He was hopelessly ineffective; he was not able to keep pace with life.

These ideas constituted an injury to his self-esteem and self-identity that he could not sustain. He started to think irrationally, and his thoughts became disorganized. He saw the world in an unusual way – as going fast, so fast that he could not cope with its movement. The diffuse and yet all-pervasive feeling of inadequacy was metaphorically changed by the illness into his sensation of not being able, in a physical sense, to keep up with the movement of the world. The accident with the car probably provided the idea of movement. Peculiar ideas (like that of his aunt calling me) were clearly in full swing a few hours after the beginning of the illness, and irrational concepts were developing in rapid sequence. He already saw things in a different, confusing way and was making an attempt to reinterpret reality.

Some readers might say, and rightly so, that many people would not have developed schizophrenia just because of a minor accident like the one that had occurred. Even when an accident caps a series of unpleasant and demoralizing life experiences, most people are able to take the event in their stride. Some would advance the hypothesis that the veteran's illness was the result of a bio-chemical alteration of the brain, and that the accident was just the straw that broke the camel's back.

At this point I do not wish to enter into a discussion of the causation of schizophrenia. This is a complicated subject that will be examined later in the book. With regard to this patient, however, we can say that he very probably had an unusual sensitivity that made him less fit to cope with some circumstances, more reactive to some situations. As we shall see later, we could even say that during very unpleasant experiences he was prone to biochemical reactions in the brain in quantities that differ from those in the average person. However, many other particulars cannot be discounted. Whatever the patient's special sensitivity or vulnerability, it would not have been enough to provoke the disorder had it not been allowed to build up to a crescendo of negative dispositions toward life. The adverse psychological factors in their turn increased the sensitivity and vulnerability of the patient.

We also cannot consider it coincidental that the attack of the illness started the day of the accident. Would any other kind of accident have been able to discharge the attack that day? For instance, if the patient had slipped on the sidewalk and fallen to the ground, breaking a leg, would he have become schizophrenic? The answer is no. Slipping on the sidewalk and breaking a leg would not have the same significance for him. The psychological traumatic accident had to be one that could be interpreted as proof of his inadequacy and, therefore, one that would produce an injury to his self-esteem. The patient had appeared very vulnerable the first two times I had seen him. I recognized in his insecurity signs of trouble to come, and I had urged him to continue treatment; but I was not able to overcome the influence of his relatives or of his own wishes.

This case is illustrative on many counts. First of all, did I make some mistakes? I think now that I should have been much firmer in recommending continuation of treatment, in spite of strong opposition. I must say, however, that more than thirty years ago, when this episode took place, I acted in accordance with the knowledge available at the time. Moreover, we know that even in cases in which we recognize signs of trouble to come, the trouble may not materialize. I also felt then, as I do now, that a psychiatrist – even when he sees signs of danger – can only make recommendations and must leave the final decision to the patient and his nearest relatives. If the patient is not able to decide for himself, the family must carefully follow the recommendations of the psychiatrist, unless there are strong and persuasive reasons for doing otherwise. In this case, the schizophrenic attack could have been prevented if the patient had continued treatment. Whatever constitutional weakness he had, it was not conspicuous. Nobody ever suspected that there was anything drastically wrong with this young man until he became ill. The course toward schizophrenia could also have been altered long ago, when he was an adolescent, if something had been done to make him change his image of himself.

Let us take again the example of Joseph Monrot, whom we mentioned in Chapter 1. Everyone was stunned at the suddenness of his breakdown, yet many people had recognized that he was discontented. His family had seen that he tried to control his discontent and not talk about it, as if he were ashamed of it. His parents and sister had noticed that it had become harder and harder for him to get up in the morning, but no one realized that what was really becoming harder and harder for Joseph was to face the day. Then one morning the alarm clock seemed to ring so loudly that he felt he had to get up no matter how hard the day would be. Everybody had to get up. The alarm clock woke up the whole city, woke it up to a harsh, horrible reality. His parents had noticed a change in him, but they did not want to invade his privacy. They believed they had no right to inquire, and they never found out what was troubling him. Underlying Joseph's inability to face the day was the long, sad history concealed within him. His parents' desire not to 'invade his privacy' was a rationalization; they did not feel close enough to him to ask personal questions.

Ann Marie Rufell had mentioned to her parents that she felt undesirable, that no man would ever love and marry her, that she would never be able to find an occupation commensurate with her aspirations. But her remarks were always interpreted by her family as being pessimistic, ridiculously inappropriate to the circumstances, and not worthy of serious consideration. Thus Ann Marie kept within herself everything that was disturbing. She did not allow warning signals to come to the surface. They were unpleasant, not only to others but also to herself, and she did not want to hear them.

Acute Signs

In this chapter I shall discuss other examples of situations in which warning signals of schizophrenia to come develop acutely, and some in which they manifest themselves slowly. I shall also describe some symptoms that are mistaken for schizophrenia and that unnecessarily frighten relatives.

A situation that I have seen occur many times is the following. A freshman in college calls his parents. He does not feel well; he has a feeling that he cannot make it in college. He feels like he is 'cracking up, going to pieces.' How is a parent to respond? Is the telephone call to be interpreted as a real warning that the student is 'going to pieces,' as an omen of impending schizophrenia? Not necessarily. Parents know that youngsters who are away from home for the first time may have considerable difficulty in adjusting to a new environment, one in which they have to take care of themselves, make new friends, and meet difficult academic requirements. The parent should warmly reassure the son or daughter and explain that these difficulties are common and have to be overcome gradually. The parent should also tell the student to call again soon and should himself or herself call the following day to verify that the acute anxiety is over.

But if the anxiety is not over, if it has unreasonably increased, if the student has called again and again with a tone of alarm, and if he continues to insist that he feels like he is cracking up, his words must be considered an appeal, a message that perhaps he has a serious doubt as to whether he is able to cope with a situation so loaded with anxiety at this point, when he is away from home for the first time. He may have seemed to manage all right at home and to be ready for college, but he gave that impression only in the protective environment of the family, where mother and father took care of many things for him.

There are several courses of action – for instance, to ask a friend or acquaintance who lives near the college to visit the student, give whatever reassurance he can, and report his appraisal of the situation to the parents. The most effective course of action, however, is for mother or father (or both) to see the student immediately and perhaps stay with him for two or three days to assess the matter. If he only needs some reassurance, some affection from the parents he misses so much, some guidance on how to handle all the new things he has to contend with, and if he feels his peace of mind is restored, the parents should leave him, glad that they have accomplished something very important.

But if the student persists in his state of anxiety and is very reluctant to let the parents go, if his uncertainty seems to escalate, and if, when the parents try to reassure him, he continuously contradicts them and tries to demonstrate that their reassurance is not valid because there are additional threats to his security, the parents should seriously consider taking the student back home, preferably after having consulted a professional.

This does not mean that the youngster has to forgo a college education. It may only have to be postponed, possibly for as little as six months, during which the student may undergo psychotherapy and analyze the causes of his anxiety. It is always a serious decision to interrupt college studies, serious for the parents as well as for the student, after so many joyful preparations and promising expectations; but no matter how unpleasant, this is a decision people have to make at times in order to avert more profound problems.

At this point some readers may wonder whether I consider leaving home and going to college sufficient in itself to precipitate one of the most serious mental disorders. Of course not. More than 99 per cent of students who go to college do not undergo this state of turmoil. But in cases like the one I have described, the ground was prepared for what is called a state of preschizophrenic panic. Many circumstances, including special sequences of psychological events not previously considered harmful, and other factors (which will be considered later in this book), such as particular biochemical mechanisms of the organism or a particular sensitivity of the nervous system, may have contributed to creating a climate of insecurity and instability that has put this student at great risk. This vulnerability, not great in the home environment, has become much stronger in the new situation. Could not this vulnerability reveal itself when the young student has to cope with other difficulties?

Let us assume that the student does not continue college studies but finds a job. The job, too, constitutes a challenge. Could he not collapse in his attempt to cope with it? In other words, is the person always going to be someone who must be treated with great care and pampered, and one who must avoid any kind of stress? Not necessarily. Every case has to be examined individually.

Psychiatrists who have studied the psychology of schizophrenia realize that a certain situation, although capable of producing some stress in almost everyone, causes serious consequences in only a few people. In other words, the threshold that must be passed for a state of preschizophrenic panic to ensue is not the same for everybody. At times a low threshold can be attributed to biochemical or inherited factors; more often, to sequences of psychological events. A feeling of 'not making it' on a job, as experienced by the veteran mentioned at the beginning of this chapter or by some students in college, is particularly destructive because of the special meaning given by the patient to the event that caused that feeling. It is when the injury is a serious blow to the image one has of oneself that a state of mental disintegration is more likely to occur.

In discussing the case of the veteran, I made the comment that a certain situation is dangerous if it touches the particular vulnerability of the patient. At times the vulnerability is not detected even by a competent psychiatrist. Most of the time, however, it is not detected because the premonitory signs were ignored. At times parents do not heed these signs or refuse to see them. Their intentions are good, and their feelings are understandable. It is painful for a parent to admit that, at a time when friends of their children are ready for college, their own child is not. They ignore the appeals for help. There are many possible consequences: the student may eventually become ill, or he may search for escapes to avoid the anxiety. Two escapes are relatively common. The first is sexual behavior that does not fit with the patient's previous personality, principles, or aims and leads to greater dissatisfaction. The second is the immoderate use not only of marijuana or hashish but also possibly of mescaline or LSD. Whereas the first escape, objectionable as it is to most parents, may delay the occurrence of a psychosis, the second may hasten it.

Being away from home for any reason – not only to pursue college studies – may acutely increase the risk of schizophrenia.

The panic I have described in college students occurs at least as frequently in youngsters who are away at camp. Its occurrence in camp is less dangerous, however, for two reasons. First, the camper has not reached the age at which schizophrenia is likely to occur. As a rule, the personality has not yet developed the sophistication to experience the deep conflicts that can lead to schizophrenia. Second, because of the younger age of the camper and because of the lesser significance given to being in camp as compared to being in college, parents more readily take the child back home if necessary.

Occasionally youngsters who are abroad experience pangs of nostalgia, feel out of place in a foreign country, and long to return home. Staying in a foreign place may be felt as being distant from or out of touch with familiar people, and these feelings may bring about fear. If the unrest continues, the young people should be advised to return home at the earliest opportunity.

Another condition that acutely increases an often unsuspected vulnerability to schizophrenia is childbirth. Childbirth is an event generally anticipated with joy. The woman may feel that her feminine identity will come to the fore when she has given birth, that her maternal love will permit the demonstration of a rich dimension of her personality. When the child arrives, however, the reality may be completely different. In such cases, about three days after the birth the mother starts to feel anxious, suspicious, excited; then she becomes irrational and incoherent in a typically schizophrenic manner. Fortunately these cases are not numerous, but in these, too, small premonitory signs could have revealed that the woman was not prepared for childbirth and motherhood, and trouble could have been averted.

Perhaps the woman yielded to pressure from her husband, her parents, her parents-in-law, or from society to become a mother, but in reality she has serious doubts. Will she be a good mother? Is she making an unconscious comparison between her mother and herself? Will she be able to be as good a mother as her mother was? Or, more frequently, will she be as bad a mother to her child as she thinks her mother was to her? Does she really want a child? Does she really want to give up her career in order to take care of her child? She believes she does not. She really did not want to be a mother; she thinks she will not be able to be a good mother. She sees herself as a woman who failed, or even as a monster who cannot be a mother.

Distortions, inappropriate apprehensions, exaggerations, and misconceptions may lead her to a state of despair, which makes her very vulnerable to mental illness, either deep depression or schizophrenia. Had she revealed her uncertainty to a professional therapist before becoming pregnant, or even while she was pregnant, she would have been properly guided and the illness, most probably, would have been averted. Even a frank discussion with her husband or with a close friend would have helped. Many women do not have these conflicts; some have them but are able to master them. A few, however, for whatever biochemical or psychological reasons, cannot master them. The conflicts grow, after childbirth, when the patient is confronted with the child.

If we are able to remove or modify the conditions that cause stress and increase the vulnerability of the patient, we may avert the illness. If we try to remove the conditions after the illness has started, we may not necessarily be successful in making the illness disappear. Once the illness has begun, much more is required than the removal of the stressful situation. An elaborate course of treatment, often requiring long psychotherapy and drug therapy, is necessary to neutralize or overcome the abnormal functioning of the mind.

There is a small minority of professional people who believe it is better to go through a schizophrenic episode and recover than not to have it at all and retain the illness in a latent state. An outbreak of illness, they believe, strengthens the personality. I do not agree at all with this point of view. Although it is true that some patients develop stronger personalities as a result of the illness and especially of the treatment, this outcome is uncertain. The risk remains great. The best thing we can do in relation to schizophrenia is to prevent the disorder, as we shall see in greater detail in Chapter 11.

Insidious and Slowly Developing Signs

So far I have described cases in which warning signs of schizophrenia present themselves acutely, suddenly, often as a consequence of a special and unusual occurrence, and with manifestations that are rather easy to detect.

In most cases, however, these warning signals are less obvious and develop over a long period of time. For the sake of accuracy, I must mention that these insidious and slowly developing signs often existed even in those cases that I have already described, in which acute precipitating factors were eventually added. I shall give a brief account now of these less obvious signals. (This matter will be examined again in a later chapter devoted to the prevention of schizophrenia.)

First I want to clarify the important fact that none of these indications are sure signs, or even presumptive signs, of schizophrenia. As a matter of fact, in most persons who exhibit these characteristics schizophrenia never develops. However, we must say that in comparison with that for the general population, the risk of schizophrenia for these people is many times greater. I shall indicate several possibilities, ranging from the most to the least dangerous.

1. A remarkable change in the personality of the person has occurred. At times the change has taken place so slowly that people who live with the person have not noticed it. A relative or a friend who lives in another city and sees the patient again after a relatively long time realizes that he does not seem to be the same person. He is less alert, more hesitant, less effective. If he had been a good student, now he is much less diligent and in danger of failing or dropping out of school. He appears disinterested in many things that were formerly of the utmost concern.

In other cases the opposite occurs. The patient is much more outgoing, even impertinent. While he had been rather shy and very conservative in some ways – in his sexual attitudes, for instance – he may now proposition others or provoke them with suggestive words or gestures. In some cases the person frankly tells his family and friends that he cannot control his impulses. He has to carry out some actions for which he must feel responsible, and yet he feels that it is not really he who has initiated these acts. Some of these patients are at times confused with 'psychopaths' or 'sociopaths' – people with a personality disorder that causes them to give vent to antisocial behavior, such as stealing, in order to satisfy their wishes. The people who are at high risk for schizophrenia, however, are not psychopaths; even if they do become schizophrenic, their chance for recovery is better than if they were psychopaths.

2. The person is restless, always on the go; asks many needless questions; becomes very sensitive; and misinterprets or sees negative allusions in innocent remarks made by members of the family or others. For instance, if a mother asks her daughter why she wore a particular dress that day, the daughter might interpret her mother's remark as an unbearable criticism, an injury to her self-esteem, as if the mother had implied, 'How inappropriate to wear that dress.' What is particularly disturbing is the fact that these misunderstandings occur more and more frequently, and especially in situations in which nobody could have anticipated them.

Particular (and mistaken) intentions are attributed to people. At times these misunderstandings occur because of poor communication between people who do not accept one another fully. For instance, misinterpretations occur frequently between mothers-in-law and daughters-in-law or between stepmothers and stepchildren, but less frequently between stepfathers and step-children. However, if the misunderstandings repeat themselves to the point of absurdity, suspicions of trouble to come should arise.

For instance, a seventeen-year-old girl thought that her step-mother played Mozart and Vivaldi on the stereo purposely to annoy her. The stepmother should know that she liked only rock music. This little episode tells us many things. Of course, behind this misinterpretation – of an evil intention attributed to the stepmother – was the rivalry with the stepmother, the resentment that the father had married again shortly after the death of the girl's mother. It is also possible that the stepmother was resentful of the stepdaughter and disregarded her needs and wishes – for example the playing of some rock music at times. However, the fact that the young girl attributed this bad intention to the stepmother was beyond ordinary misunderstanding and should have been given particular attention.

At times these misunderstandings occur at work. The person feels that the boss is unfair, demands too much, or makes inappropriate comments.

3. A pattern that used to be much more common but that is still frequent today consists of a gradual withdrawal from life. The person becomes more and more reserved, closed in on himself, a shut-in personality. In some cases he seems to make an effort to appear as inconspicuous as possible. It is as if he were living in an ivory tower, or as if a barrier were separating him from the rest of the world. He seems to be less spontaneous or even indifferent to what goes on and acts as if he wanted to reduce his needs, his contacts with others, and his own activities to the very minimum. In some cases in which the individual retains some interpersonal relations, he seems to allow himself to be manipulated by others.

4. The person is very insecure and anxious. Although he has always been very worried, now the anxiety assumes an element of despair. The person is less and less hopeful about succeeding in anything. He contemplates the possibility that nothing he does will work out. He feels he may fail in everything. He does not even talk about it, because people may misunderstand him. In fact, people think that he is a pessimistic or depressed person who has lost hope. But the truth is that he is not depressed; he has not given up. Because he has not given up, however, he has to pay the high price of experiencing tremendous anxiety. At times he seems anxious about everything; he may even experience irrational fears.

Two conditions that should worry parents or relatives are excessive use of alcohol, to the point of repeated intoxication, and use of psychedelic drugs.

Excessive use of alcohol is always to be avoided, but in the cases we are discussing, the patient has more than an alcohol problem. Without realizing it, the person wants to cover up or dispel, by the use of alcohol, a state of anxiety that is so strong as to be a forerunner of schizophrenia. Psychedelic drugs, too, can be used as escapes, but the escapes they offer are illusory. The anxiety has to be dealt with appropriately, often with professional help.

The warning signs that I have mentioned so far are particularly frequent in people in the late teens through the early thirties. However, it is important to detect suspicious signs in early adolescence and in childhood, when the possibility of schizophrenia is, as a rule, still remote.

Early signs of trouble to come are not always detected in adolescence. Adolescence is an age whose impact is felt throughout the whole life of the individual. Whereas early psychoanalytic research gave almost exclusive importance to childhood as the age that, to a large extent, determines any subsequent developmental stage, present research gives great importance also to adolescence in the shaping of the personality. Adolescence is a period of life that presents the most varied characteristics and patterns of behavior – from a great desire to imitate the adults that the youngster admires to a strong and repeated effort to be different, to follow a completely unusual, even unconventional and wild course of life. These great variations are not necessarily preschizophrenic, although they may resemble the deviations that occur in schizophrenia. There are some theorists, as a matter of fact, who interpret schizophrenia as a stage of growth similar to adolescence. Others consider adolescence a type of schizophrenia from which most of us recover. To me these statements seem misleading and at best metaphorical. It is true that adolescence is an age during which new horizons open up and new feelings develop; consequently, it is a stage of development in which states of uncertainty, rebelliousness, and even unusual patterns of behavior occur. All this may be reminiscent of schizophrenia, but whereas adolescence leads to personality growth, even in stormy periods, schizophrenia generally leads to a disintegration or restriction of life.

There are cases in which the adolescent appears very eager to make interpersonal contacts, eager to a frenzied extent. Later, this sudden and insatiable hunger for new experiences is followed by a rapid dropping of social contacts, only to be renewed still later in a repetitive cycle. Such patterns of behavior constitute legitimate reasons for concern. We must ascertain whether this endless search is a real quest for growth and an exploration of life or an indication that the youngster cannot accept what he receives or is unable to make appropriate use of it. In case of doubt, professional consultation is advisable.

At times premonitory signs occur much earlier. Some youngsters who develop surprising attacks of schizophrenia in late adolescence have always been 'good children' who very seldom cried, lied, or had temper tantrums. They never caused their parents any trouble; they always obeyed, always went along with whatever demands were made on them. When this type of behavior persists and becomes conspicuous for its passivity, the alert parent should think about whether the child is really at peace with himself, or whether he is unwilling to dare. Does he comply in order to please, or in order not to displease? Is he really a person who is content, or one who does not want to show his discontent? Often under the label of 'good boy' or 'good girl' is hidden a great deal of suffering. A picture of passive acceptance of life as it is, without any spark of individuality and originality, is a condition that requires further investigation.

False Signs

There are some behaviors and habits that may scare parents but should not. It is important to mention the most common of them. One seems hardly worth noting because today almost everybody knows that the old belief has no validity whatsoever. And yet in many backward areas of the world the idea persists that excessive masturbation leads to schizophrenia or is a sign of oncoming schizophrenia. Even in some textbooks of psychiatry published as late as the beginning of this century, the idea was repeatedly expressed that excessive masturbation leads to mental illness. If there are still some parents today who accept this, they should try to overcome the belief, which is based on a tradition many centuries old, but they should not feel embarrassed to have believed it.

Strangely enough, a condition that occasionally alarms some people and makes them think of schizophrenia is gullibility. On rare occasions scared parents consult psychiatrists because their youngsters profess to believe in such things as flying saucers, interplanetary communication, reincarnation, astrology, communication with ghosts, and the like. The possibility that such thoughts may be irrational and indicative of schizophrenia has to be taken into consideration. However, it is generally easy to determine whether the child has been influenced by some special groups or by what he has read in newspapers, magazines, or books or has seen in science fiction movies or on television. Gullibility may be the result of several different conditions. Among the most common is the need to belong to, or to be accepted by, a group – for instance, a group that believes in astrology, supernatural powers, or exotic cults. At times gullibility is based on a state of insecurity that hinders critical faculties and promotes suggestibility and indoctrination. Much less frequently, a limited intellectual endowment is responsible for credulity. On the other hand, gullibility may even be a quality necessary for creativity. Creative people tend to keep their minds open even for hard-to-believe possibilities; they let their thinking and imagination rove along unusual and strange lines. They dismiss the incredible idea only when it has been definitely proven wrong.

The reference to creativity leads me to discuss related problems. Many youngsters, especially adolescents, present a group of characteristics that often worry parents and friends unnecessarily. These young people like to be alone for a few hours every day; they tend to daydream, read, or think a great deal instead of associating with peers; they notice coincidences or similarities between apparently unrelated things; and they have a rich fantasy life. Actually, the majority of these youngsters are potentially creative. Some qualities, like lack of gregariousness, aloneness, and daydreaming are ways that permit them to roam outside the beaten path. Although most parents want their children to be creative, they seem to encourage popularity and being like other boys and girls, and they are very concerned with what seems to them excessive loafing, daydreaming, introversion, and even signs of schizophrenia to come. This line of thinking is wrong, of course. The aloneness of the potentially creative person is different from the painful detachment of the youngster who withdraws from his environment. The former type of behavior is motivated by the desire to focus on the richness of one's inner life and resources, the latter by fear and discomfort found in interpersonal relations.

Some parents report completely different observations to doctors. They say that there seemed to be something wrong with the child from the very moment of birth. The baby appeared nervous, cried all the time, had feeding problems, and so on. Later, but still early in childhood, he was impossible to take care of. 'Even a saint would not have been able to take care of him.' Some parents are afraid that these children are candidates for schizophrenia. Most probably, the majority of these so-called impossible children are children with minimal brain damage who are consequently hyperactive. They move furniture, open drawers, touch everything, are always on the go. Fortunately, most of these children outgrow their symptoms later in childhood or in adolescence. While many parents are able to adjust to these deviations of the child, especially with medical guidance, others are not. Those who do not adjust become increasingly alarmed and anxious and respond to their anxiety not with greater care but with poor parenting. A vicious circle of anxiety from child to parent and back from the parent to child results. Unless corrected, this state of affairs may lead to troubles that outweigh by far the original ones caused by minimal brain damage and in some rare cases may even lead to schizophrenia. With proper treatment practically all these children overcome their problems and have a normal adult life.

Phobias (that is, irrational fears such as being afraid of the dark, of being alone in a room, of being bitten by animals, of being separated from mother as when going to school) are generally not conducive to schizophrenia. However, they do require medical attention. Phobias become signs of more serious disturbances when the feared object is not a thing, an animal, or a special situation, but a human being. Irrational fears are also a matter of more serious concern when they are accompanied by other symptoms, such as withdrawal and suspiciousness.

Other signs that occasionally concern parents are the little rituals children indulge in. For instance, before going to bed a child may have to put the pillow in a special position. When he walks on the stairs he may have to skip every second step or avoid any line on the floor and so on. Many children, during a stage of their development, have these little obsessive-compulsive symptoms, which are not an indication of schizophrenia to come. Nonetheless, a marked obsessive-compulsive condition requires medical attention.

Conclusions

To summarize, in this chapter we have discussed signs that indicate that a person's risk of schizophrenia is increased in comparison to that of the general population. We have also discussed other symptoms that, although they are distressing and require medical attention, are not related to schizophrenia. Finally, we have reviewed some characteristics that, although they cause perplexity and are at times mistakenly thought to be indicative of future schizophrenia, do not indicate abnormality.

In this chapter we have also started to learn that when schizophrenia originates, generally in early adulthood, it is not a completely new development but the continuation of an abnormal course of events that existed below the level of awareness of the family and of the patient himself. Definite indications or tests to detect the presence or the future emergence of schizophrenia – similar to laboratory tests done on blood and urine to determine metabolic disorders, blood diseases, or infections – do not exist.

Many theorists consider schizophrenia a failure of vast proportions in relinquishing modes of functioning normal to childhood. In other words, schizophrenia would be a failure to 'grow up.' This belief is seemingly supported by the fact that when the illness has started, there is a readoption of immature ways of thinking and acting similar to those appearing in childhood. However, it would be completely wrong to consider the schizophrenic as somebody who remains immature, or who is unable to progress beyond a childhood level.

Although some of these patients retain some immature traits, most of them are quite advanced psychologically before they become ill; even when they are ill, they manifest a great deal of maturity, mixed with some returning immature traits.

At this point we can add to the definition of schizophrenia given in the previous chapter and state that it is a condition with a long history that predates its apparent onset.

3. A Description of Schizophrenia

In this chapter we shall see not only how schizophrenia appears in the eye of the observer, but also how it is experienced by the patient as he undergoes psychological transformation. Schizophrenia has a thousand faces; we cannot possibly describe all its aspects. In spite of the enormous diversity of the symptomatology, however, psychiatrists have distinguished several different types, and we shall describe the most common of them. Before doing so, let us look at a general picture.

The schizophrenic illness generally manifests itself in two major ways. One is characterized by a psychological withdrawal, which reflects the patient's attitude toward the world: the infinite fear of the world, the gigantic distrust of people, the total desire to escape from everything. Often this desire to escape is justified by the patient with the thought or feeling that the world does not deserve to be looked at or to be joined; it is not worthy of his participation in it. At times he stares vacantly, as if he did not want to focus his eyes on the terrible things he sees all around.

The other major way is characterized by what psychiatrists, using a term coined by Freud, call *projection*. A cluster or system of false beliefs possesses the patient. Terrible dangers are near; persecutors are plotting in a myriad of possible ways. The perils are experienced intensely as if they were real, and the patient lives them as agonizing truth.

Let us examine these two pictures in greater detail. How does each originate?

The patient, generally young (from the time of puberty to his early thirties) but less commonly of any age, has started to display unusual behavior. As we have seen in Chapter 2, some unconventional traits may have appeared earlier, but they remained unnoticed or were disregarded. Now they become conspicuous and impose themselves, although at times they may admit of plausible explanations. Some important decisions that the patient has recently made seem strange, although again in some cases they can be justified. For instance, a college student may drop out of school suddenly, thinking he cannot make it in his studies. A worker may feel that the boss or the other workers are unfair to him, are not well disposed toward him, or are disrespectful. They want to get him into trouble, put him in a bad light, or give him a difficult assignment. They dislike him for definite or, more often, indefinite reasons. In some cases the patient refuses to go to work and becomes preoccupied with seemingly unimportant matters. These unusual traits eventually become striking, at times in a slow, insidious, progressive way; at other times more acutely, as in the two patients mentioned at the beginning of Chapter 1. As we shall study in greater detail in Chapter 4, in many cases the particular type of personality that the family had recognized in the patient before he became ill blended almost imperceptibly with the manifestation of the illness, so that it becomes impossible to determine when the illness actually started.

In some cases the illness begins with a period of confusion, excitement, and agitation. The patient seems to be eager to make contacts, to reach all the people he knows, to reconnect himself with what seems to him an escaping world. He searches for something that he cannot find. But at times he does not even know that he searches. He wants to be active and manifests an intensified hunger for life, for all kinds of experiences, but his confusion is more prominent than his search. His excitement may become pronounced, his speech may lose coherence, and the abnormality becomes obvious.

In other cases the patient becomes concerned with hypochondriacal preoccupations and often refers to his numerous illnesses. At other times he is concerned with his physical appearance, the shape of his nose, his ears, his protruding teeth, breasts, hair, and so on. Again, whereas his complaints at first seem to have some plausibility, soon they reveal themselves as unfounded or as gigantic exaggerations or distortions.

In many cases the patient seems less interested in life than he used to be. He concentrates instead on some specific problems. He starts to think that certain things pertain to him or have a special meaning. These special preoccupations are called *ideas of reference.* For instance, if the patient meets a particular person on the street, he believes it was because that person was spying on him. He does not seem capable of believing that events may occur by chance or at random; they take place only because they are preordained, prearranged by people. Thus, if he happened to think about a certain subject and then sees that particular subject mentioned in the newspaper or in the movies, or hears it referred to on television or radio, he does not consider this fact as a mere coincidence, but something to be looked upon with suspicion.

Suspiciousness of other people increases. The patient thinks that they are looking at him in a peculiar way; they are making fun of him and may even be talking behind his back. He is under the influence of obscure external groups or organizations, such as some political groups, some ethnic minorities, the Mafia, or even inhabitants of other planets. 'They' make him experience peculiar sensations; 'they' make him think in a way that is foreign to his manner of thinking; 'they' use him as a guinea pig; 'they' make him act in a way over which he has no control. He does not specify who 'they' are. They are indefinite aggressive persons, either one person or a group.

Finally, the patient gives some definite interpretations to facts and things that are not supported by the observations made by other people. The house is wired; dictaphones are hidden for the purpose of registering the patient's thoughts; poison has been put in the food; telepathic or hypnotic experiments are secretly being done on him. These are false beliefs, or *delusions;* they are generally of negative character, inasmuch as they seem to convince the patient that some people or outside forces want to persecute him, injure him, or at least watch him or plan some future disturbance. There is somebody who controls, or wants to gain control of, his actions or thoughts. The patient receives special messages, often transmitted in secret codes. Words used by people acquire special meanings and appear to him to be puns or alliterations. Some patients discover puns everywhere; others give special interpretations to gestures of people they come into contact with, and even to casual or accidental sounds.

At a later stage, however, these delusions may become pleasant in content and even grandiose. The patient is a queen, a millionaire; a great actor is going to marry her. The patient may believe that he has made a great invention, discovered the secrets of the universe, or devised a philosophical system that will explain the essence of life. It is now he who, by telepathic or hypnotic means, can control other people, the weather, the stock market, the population explosion.

The way the patient perceives external stimuli is altered, too, for he hears or sees things in a distorted way. His familiar environment now appears to him strange or unusual. Things and persons have a different aspect and relate to him in a way that is different from the previous way. People change dimensions and seem unusually large or small. Also, movements are registered differently; the rhythm of life has become too fast or too slow. At times things are confused with other things (*illusions*). Persons are misidentified. Strange resemblances are observed. An old man on the street looks exactly like the patient's grandfather (maybe he is the grandfather's twin brother, whose existence was unknown to the patient).

As frequent as illusions, and in some cases more frequent, are *hallucinations*, or perceptions occurring without any stimulus in the external environment that could be responsible for them. The patient hears people talking to him or mentioning his name, yet no one speaks to him or about him. He may see people and things that are not there. In many cases hallucinations are preceded by, or may occur together with, the feeling that one's thoughts have become audible, that they can be heard by people standing nearby or even in distant places. In a very large number of cases the patient hears voices that accuse him of being a spy, a homosexual, a pervert, a murderer, and yet nobody is there to say these things. Hallucinations involve every sense, the auditory being as a rule the most common throughout the course of the disorder. Hallucinations involving smell, taste, and touch are much less frequent.

At times the general behavior and demeanor of the patient retain a normal aspect, and the only apparent symptoms are the abnormal ideas. On the other hand, in many cases the appearance of the patient seems unusual and graceless, because the patient makes grimaces, or mouths words, or moves his lips oddly, or indulges in strange movements that are stereotyped and manneristic, affecting strange, theatrical, or outlandish behavior. In some other cases, he makes impulsive gestures, crying, screaming, or roaring with laughter.

In some cases the patient behaves in a way that is in striking contrast to his previous habits. Whereas before he was sexually reserved, now he becomes daring and given to unconventional behavior. He may even make sexual advances in the most inappropriate and unacceptable ways. If before he was submissive or self-effacing, he may become querulous, antagonistic, even belligerent. Many patients are unable to pay attention when they talk with others. They repeat the same question as if they had not heard the answer already given.

Emotionally the patient seems quite different. He may readily become anxious, fearful, angry, suspicious, cynical. At times he seems quite unemotional, even when he speaks about matters that would stir the emotions of other people. Often apparent indifference or complete apathy can be detected.

In other cases the picture consists mainly of the general withdrawal that we have already mentioned. The patient seems to have lost not only his understanding of but also his interest in and participation in reality. He is in a shell, his own private little world. His activities are reduced to a minimum and are often performed in a routine, stereotyped manner. Often he has to be pushed to do things. He may be so unwilling to act that he becomes neglectful of his personal appearance. Special types of schizophrenia will be described later in this chapter.

Schizophrenia from Different Perspectives

At this juncture it is important to consider what has happened from the point of view of the family and of the patient himself. The family is at first only surprised. Some characteristics of the patient appear somewhat peculiar but are thought to be only expressions of the individuality of the patient, or of his desire to be different or self-assertive. Then what at first seemed an idiosyncratic attitude of the patient becomes for him a cosmic theme. At this point the family becomes bewildered. It dawns on them that the patient is not in a normal state, and that a doctor has to be consulted. A campaign is begun to convince the patient to consult a doctor.

If the members of the family are knowledgeable about schizophrenia, at this point they must try to understand that there is a need for the patient to see the world in a different way. There is no point in trying to convince him that he is wrong, and even worse is it to ridicule him for his 'bizarre' way of thinking. The family members may say something like this: 'John, there must be a reason for your seeing things that we don't see. Perhaps an expert in this matter may help all of us to find the reason.'

The description given in the previous section is predominantly that of an observer, or even of an examiner who asked the patient to describe what happened to him. The examiner, however, has maintained his objectivity or a preliminary clinical distance and has not tried, so far, to enter the mind of the patient.

Although the patient has undergone a change that has made him become ill, he does not realize that a transformation has taken place *within him*. He believes instead that the outside world has changed. To use an analogy – but a very imperfect one – he is like a person who wears a pair of glasses with lenses that distort what he sees. This person does not know that he is wearing those particular glasses and believes that what he sees corresponds to reality. The alteration in the schizophrenic's world involves not only what the patient sees and hears, but especially what has to be assessed by his new way of reasoning and colored by his emotions.

In typical acute cases the initial stage of the illness can be divided into three substages. The first is characterized by an extreme feeling of anxiety that seems to come from nowhere. In the second substage many things happen that are all in a state of confusion. At times some plausible ideas achieve predominance in the patient's mind. He is not able to pay attention to other things or to answer questions that are not directly related to his dominant idea. He has feelings of discomfort. He wants very badly to be reassured, but nobody seems able to help him. He does not even hear the answers to his questions, so preoccupied is he. He thus repeats the same question many times and seems to suffer a great deal.

At times he succeeds in snapping out of this state of torment and returning to his normal condition. In some cases he may even feel better for a few hours or days, but then the panic returns, even stronger than before. The patient has the feeling that something terrible is happening to him. Maybe he is becoming insane. A little later he feels that other people think he may be insane. He has the sensation that he is losing a battle, an unknown battle. He becomes more and more discouraged. His confusion and fright become greater and greater; they overcome and submerge him, like large waves. Things seem peculiar; they acquire a different perceptual quality and an obscure meaning. At times the patient finds himself indulging in fantasies that he himself recognizes as false, and yet they are so vivid that they seem real. He tries to find an explanation for all this, but he cannot. In many cases the patient feels that people are acting out a play to confuse him. The world becomes a big stage.

In typical cases, after this period of confusion, a third substage occurs during which the patient feels that everything is clear. All of a sudden he experiences a flash of understanding. The light has come back. Things that appeared confused and obscure have a meaning, a purpose. He feels exceptionally lucid. He understands everything now; the strange events were not accidental, but purposely arranged. Somebody, somewhere, is after him, against him. From now on, and for a long time, the patient will try to demonstrate logically what seems evident to him. He develops the phenomenon that I have called *psychotic insight.* The illness is now well established in a paranoid pattern.

Why should we call this phenomenon psychotic insight? Insight means a sudden discovery of relationships and meanings between different things and facts. Certain things that before appeared to the patient as disconnected and unrelated are now seen as parts of a whole. But the insight is psychotic because only the patient sees these connections. He 'puts two and two together'; he is able to 'assemble the various pieces of a jigsaw puzzle.' But only he is able to detect the puzzle. He is able to see the world in a different way because he adopts new ways of thinking. He abandons logical thinking and adopts new patterns that we shall describe later. He feels that he has never thought as clearly and effectively as now. Such an impression is occasionally conveyed to the layman.

It is important to stress that the patient often does not acquire these new and abnormal ways of interpreting reality without first putting up a fight within himself. When this new way of thinking lurks in the background and threatens to come to the surface, the patient at first tries to resist it. He feels a struggle within himself that is experienced as an 'attempt to resist a tendency to give in.' The patient, however, is afraid that sooner or later he will succumb. We have already referred to the fact that he feels engaged in an unsuccessful battle. On the other hand, succumbing seems a pleasant temptation because it may bring relief to a state of confusion. Psychiatrist W. J. Stein has described the patient in this substage as follows: 'Now, even though he has this sense of utter powerlessness or of being a passive observer of his own destruction, he still from time to time makes abortive attempts to resist dying, just as a drowning man who cannot swim nevertheless struggles frantically.'

When the patient finally succumbs and reaches psychotic insight, the opposite process occurs: he searches actively for evidence that will support his suspicions, and he sharpens his senses. If a noise is heard, if an acquaintance uses a special word, if a strange man is walking up and down the street, all this is corroborative evidence that what he thinks is true.

At other times this psychotic insight manifests itself in a different way. The patient does not attempt to demonstrate the validity of his ideas. He 'knows'; that is enough. His knowledge comes from an inner, unchallenged certitude that does not require demonstration. '*He knows.*'

Now, all this cannot be accepted at face value; it requires psychological interpretation. Before proceeding to advance such interpretation, I must point out, however, that the psychological interpretations, even when entirely correct, do not explain the totality of the schizophrenic picture. What I mean is this. The patient has a strong psychological need that he must satisfy: He must solve his psychological problems. He attempts to do so through his symptoms. However, he would probably not attempt to solve his problems in this abnormal way if he were not inclined to do so by a biological predisposition, or an unusual conglomeration of psychological factors, or a mixture of physical and psychological factors. At any rate, even if these factors are necessary, it is important to understand the psychological need for the symptoms.

An example from general medicine may help to explain. Fever is often a symptom of an infectious disease. However, although it is a symptom of abnormality, fever has a useful function. It is an attempt of the organism to combat the disease itself. By raising the body's temperature, the organism fights microorganisms or their products (toxins) that have invaded the body and made it sick. In schizophrenia, too, symptoms may have a useful function, although there is no invasion of microorganisms. The invaders are instead feelings about one's self, one's future, life, the world in relation to the patient.

The picture that we have described in the previous pages, although a general one, is more typical of the paranoid type of schizophrenia. What functions do these symptoms have, which is to say, what do these symptoms mean? For instance, the feeling of being accused? The tendency of the patient to blame others, either specific individuals or groups of people who cannot easily be identified? This is the mechanism of projection, to which we have already referred. Projection is another word for externalization. Through projection, a psychological problem of conflict that exists *inside* the patient is instead attributed by the patient to the external world.

Before the patient became obviously ill, he was not really well but had already developed serious psychological problems. He had very low self-esteem. He considered himself inadequate, worthless, awkward, unloved and unlovable, unaccepted and unacceptable. He blamed himself for being inadequate or inherently inferior, for not having done what he should to improve himself. He thought people were justified in having a bad opinion of him. Although most of the time he tried to deny this vision of himself and even to suppress it from consciousness, the time comes when he can no longer do so. He externalizes in a way that is not supported by logic. No longer does he accuse himself; the accusation now comes from others. In order to make this shift, he has to resort to a primitive way of thinking that, as we shall see later in greater detail, is not very accurate. The special thinking appears to us to be exaggerations and distortions; the patient makes connections by analogies and confuses analogies with identities. Thus these mysterious, imaginary persons who accuse the patient do not call him 'inadequate, unlovable, neglectful,' but in the imagination of the patient they amplify the accusation to the point of calling him 'pervert, spy, murderer, prostitute.' This symptom is one of the mechanisms that Freud called *defenses*.

For a nonprofessional person who has not studied psycho-dynamic psychiatry, it is difficult to understand how such symptoms can be called defenses or be considered useful. Isn't it an offense, rather than a defense, to be accused in such a manner, or to be the object of a conspiracy or persecution? It is, and indeed the patient who feels victimized in this way suffers a great deal. However, he no longer accuses himself. Now he has a high opinion of himself. He is a martyr, the innocent victim of the malevolence of other people. He could no longer tolerate having such low self-esteem. It was a feeling that was injuring his inner self. In order to remove this injury, he has adopted a mechanism that permits him to barter this inner injury for a different one that comes from the external world. The external threat may be harmful, but it does not lower the opinion that the patient has of himself.

Naturally this mechanism of projection is an *abnormal* one. The fact that the patient wanted to believe in an external threat, rather than an inner one that he was unable to face, is not enough to activate the mechanism of projections. As we shall see in Chapter 5, other factors may also be necessary. But no matter what is the cause or combination of causes necessary for the projection, it is important to remember that the symptom has a meaning, a meaning given to the patient by its function or alleged function. Of course, it is important to find out why the patient, prior to his becoming manifestly ill, had such a low opinion of himself, but we shall not pursue this matter now.

The Various Types of Schizophrenia

As we have mentioned, cases of schizophrenia have been classified in many ways, according to the main features that they present. In practice we find many mixed cases that do not fit any classification perfectly. Here we shall discuss the four main types, which have been described since the time of Emil Kraepelin, the psychiatrist who first reported schizophrenia in the medical literature, naming it *dementia praecox.* (The name *schizophrenia* was coined by the Swiss psychiatrist Eugen Bleuler.) To these four main types we shall add a fifth one, now more common than in previous times: the schizoaffective.

The Paranoid Type

Patients suffering from the paranoid type of schizophrenia constitute the largest group. Fundamentally, they present the picture described in the first section of this chapter with some additional characteristics of their own. Although many cases occur as early as puberty, they can be found even in the fourth and fifth decade of life.

Paranoid patients are as a rule more intelligent than the others. From the beginnings of the illness, they are suspicious and bound to misinterpret things and events in a way disparaging to themselves. For the paranoid schizophrenic the prevailing feeling about oneself is immediately externalized and perceived as a negative appraisal that others have of the patient. This occurs in accordance with the mechanism of projection, which we have already described. For instance, a patient may consider himself clumsy and ridiculously inadequate. He then develops the impression that people are laughing at him. The impression soon becomes certainty. He is sure they think he is no good, a misfit. But to be no good and a misfit for him means to be homosexual. That is why they refer to him as 'she.' For instance, the patient hears co-workers saying, 'She is not doing her work as she should.' He believes they use the word 'she' because they think the patient is not a man.

The phenomenon of *spreading of meaning* is common. A particular meaning is given to many things because the environment is reinterpreted to accommodate the basic ideas of the patient.

Not only does the patient claim that others accuse him of the traits he does not like in himself, but also he eventually ascribes to others the characteristics he cannot accept in himself. He started by being suspicious, but soon he becomes sure that other people are plotting or conspiring against him. He sees and collects the alleged evidence. He may assume the bitter, angry, antagonistic, defiant attitude of the person who is unfairly victimized, or the attitude of the submissive person who wants to be helped but does not know what to do because 'strange things are happening.'

Delusions are more frequent in the paranoid type of schizophrenia than in the other types. They may be persecutory, grandiose, hypochondriacal, or ideas of being transformed, accused, influenced, hypnotized, controlled telepathically, poisoned, made the victim of experiments, and so forth.

In a considerable number of cases, the delusions become *systematized*. This means that the patient does not accept them as random beliefs but tries to explain them more or less logically in relation to the rest of his life or what he observes in the world. A delusional system may be built around the idea that the patient is persecuted because of his ideology, philosophy, or religion. He may give his system of beliefs an apparently scientific, philosophical, or theological structure.

Delusions may have all types of content. It is impossible to enumerate all the things they can refer to. They reflect the patient's familial, cultural, and social conditions. At times the cultural influence is manifested in a paradoxical way. For instance, religion as a whole has less influence in the life of people today than in previous eras. However, there has recently been an increase in patients having grandiose delusions with religious content. The delusion of being Jesus Christ is the most common, both in Christian patients and in Jewish patients living in predominantly Christian countries. The delusion of being St Paul, the Virgin Mary, St Peter, and so forth is also fairly common. Contrary to what is written in popular books of psychiatry or frequently told in jokes, I have never seen a patient claiming to be Napoleon Bonaparte. Delusions of jealousy (beliefs that the spouse is unfaithful) are also quite common, especially later in life. They are more frequent, however, in those conditions called paranoid states, involutional paranoid states, and paranoia than in schizophrenia.

Delusions and hallucinations should not be interpreted as non-sensical beliefs or false perceptions that are to be disregarded. As we have already indicated, they have a purpose and therefore a meaning that professionals are often able to uncover. Freud demonstrated that the apparent nonsensical content of a dream has a meaning that it is important to know. Carl Jung applied to the symptoms of schizophrenia the same technique that Freud applied to dreams and became the first psychiatrist to give a full psychological interpretation to schizophrenic delusions. He wrote, 'Let the dreamer walk about and act as though he were awake, and we have at once the clinical picture of dementia praecox [schizophrenia].'

Most delusions and hallucinations can be considered as meta-phorical (especially the delusions of persecutions) or compensatory (especially the delusions of grandeur). Let us examine some examples. A patient believes that his wife is putting poison in his food. Every time he eats, he 'tastes' the poison. The patient actually believes that his wife is poisoning his life, meta-phorically. The marital situation is a very unhappy one. The patient prefers to think (or is obligated to think) that the food is poisoned. No matter how unpleasant it is to think that he may be poisoned by his wife, he can conceive the idea of the food's being poisoned more readily than that of life's being poisoned. Moreover, if he were to face the fact that his marital relationship is so disturbing, he might have to accept some responsibility for it. Maybe he is not a good husband and elicits disharmony and hostility in his wife.

Another patient has an olfactory hallucination, one of the sense of smell, on account of which he smells an unpleasant odor emanating from his body. He believes in the reality of the hallucination although he is told that nobody else smells that odor. He actually believes in his inner self that he is a rotten person, that he 'stinks' as a person, but what this symptom does for him is to remove the source of his concern from his own personality. It is much simpler or less intolerable for him to think negatively about his body.

People who believe they are Jesus Christ or the Virgin Mary are actually persons with very low self-esteem and a disastrous image of themselves. With these grandiose delusions they compensate. They become their own ideals, their symbols of perfection.

The Hebephrenic Type

It may be difficult to distinguish a hebephrenic from a paranoid. Many of the symptoms seen in the paranoid type are also seen in the hebephrenic, but they appear in a more advanced form and with a less organized and coherent structure. The most obvious difference from the paranoid type is that the hebephrenic is more confused and on the whole less able to function normally. The illness, as a rule, starts earlier in life. Some hebephrenics seem to have passed through a paranoid phase and to have moved on to a hebephrenic style of living when not treated.

The mood may be slightly depressed; more often it is one of apathy and detachment, interrupted now and then by an apparently humorous or jocular attitude. The patient often smiles in situations when it seems completely inappropriate. For instance, a question may evoke an incongruous smile instead of a verbal answer. Although at time hebephrenics can think logically, they spend a greater amount of time by far thinking in a rambling, incoherent, confused manner. In contrast to the symptoms of the paranoid type, there are no complex systematizations or connections of the delusional ideas into a philosophical or religious framework. The patient does not care, as the paranoid often does, to demonstrate that his ideas are valid. He does not need to defend himself against attacks from others. Like the paranoid he may believe he is persecuted, but he does not seem bitter about it. He has grandiose, absurd, illogically sustained delusions more often than the paranoid. The delusions of the hebephrenic are generally more out of contact with reality. They often refer to the body, which is considered to be damaged or disrupted. The patient may think that his brain has melted, that his heart has changed position, or other somatic impossibilities.

The Catatonic Type

Fortunately, the catatonic type is much less common than it used to be. After a certain period of excitement, which may even be absent in many cases and which is characterized by agitated, apparently aimless behavior, the patient slows down, sooner or later reaching a state of total passivity, withdrawal, and almost complete immobility. In the most typical cases he resembles a statue. He indeed assumes statuesque positions, which he holds for hours or days or until somebody else moves him in order to feed him, put him to bed, or take care of his physical needs. The patient seems completely detached from the world. We can tell him the most disturbing news – for instance, that a person very dear to him has suddenly died – and he will not even blink.

This detachment is only superficial. Inside him there is a volcano of emotion. Although patients have appeared to remain impassive to what was told them and have retained a flat emotionless face, many of them, at the end of the catatonic episode, have been able to repeat accurately what they heard. Thus they proved that they were very much in contact with the world but could not respond to such contact with external behavior, not even with the slight movements required to utter words.

If the patient cannot move, it is not because he is paralyzed or because there is something wrong with his motor apparatus. What is disturbed is his faculty to will, to give the parts of his body the command to move in the way required for a desired action. At times he is very obedient and suggestible, because he follows the will of somebody else. For instance, if during an examination the patient is told by the doctor, 'Show me your tongue; I want to prick it with a pin,' the patient may obligingly comply. The examiner may put the body of the patient in the most awkward positions, and the patient will remain in those positions for hours. This is the phenomenon of *waxy flexibility*.

A phenomenon that seems opposite to this suggestibility is *negativism*. Instead of doing what is requested of him, the patient does the opposite. For instance, if he is told by the examiner to show his tongue, he closes his mouth tightly or turns his face away. If he is told to stand, he assumes a reclining position. In many cases a few activities remain, but they are carried out in a routine, stereotyped manner. Any spontaneous or new activity is abolished. There are striking exceptions, however. In contrast to the usual immobility, the patient may repeatedly perform some actions that have a special meaning or purpose to him. A twenty-two-year-old girl would periodically undress herself regardless of the presence of other patients or members of the staff (of either sex).

Delusions and hallucinations are present in many cases. However, until he improves, the patient cannot communicate them to the examiner. Often these delusions and hallucinations have a cosmic quality. 'The world is being destroyed,' for example. At times the patient is able to reply to questioning, but the answers are monosyllabic: yes or no.

It is important to understand the psychological factors and childhood events that facilitate the latter occurrence of a catatonic illness. People who become catatonic are those who, early in childhood, did not develop confidence in their own actions and reliance on their capacity to make choices and decisions. In childhood these patients learned to a very marked degree the habit of following parental directions and did not practice adequately their capacity to use free will. When these people had to begin making their own choices, they found themselves doubtful, ambivalent, and unable to decide. Often the patient-to-be felt guilty about putting into practice his own wishes. After all, he might make the wrong decision. Later in life decisions that arouse anxiety to an extreme degree generally concern sexual relationships, marriage, love affairs, divorce, career changes, moves to other cities, and other similar choices.

In spite of these handicaps the patient-to-be is able to cope with most difficult situations, but sooner or later he has to face a crisis that to him seems unsurmountable. Often he fights the anxiety by resorting to obsessions and compulsions, but the anxiety is not successfully checked and the patient slips gradually into catatonic immobility.

In cases that develop very quickly, the patient lapses into complete immobility without going through interim stages. For instance, a married woman in her late twenties fell into a state of complete immobility a few minutes before she was scheduled to board a taxi that would take her to the airport. She was supposed to go to Europe to join her husband, who had gone there a year earlier. The trip would put her in a position to face him after she had become pregnant by another man and had had an abortion, at that time illegal. The situation that the patient wanted to avoid was pretending faithfulness. Such pretension was more guilt-producing than having been unfaithful.

When the catatonic does not reach complete immobility or when he improves only moderately, he still reveals in almost all his behavior the terrible uncertainty and inability to use his will. He may stop in the middle of a movement, or he may perform a series of alternating opposite movements. The desire to stay out of the world is in conflict with the desire to be involved with it, and his unusual movements and body positions are the result of both desires operating at the same time.

The chances of recovery from a catatonic episode are good, but constant attention is necessary to prevent future occurrences. Special emphasis in treatment and in home life should be given to encouraging autonomous decision-making and creating an environment in which the outcome of any decision is not viewed critically.

The Simple Type

Simple schizophrenia is the rarest form of schizophrenia found in America. Originally, simple schizophrenia was not considered a separate type, but psychiatrists found it useful to consider it apart. Unlike the other types, simple schizophrenia almost never occurs in a sudden or dramatic fashion. Instead, the development is gradual and slow. It is often impossible to find out at what point in life the illness began. Usually it appears that the problems associated with simple schizophrenia began before puberty. These problems are not clear-cut. The simple schizophrenic may become inactive and try to limit the scope of his life. He does not grow into the person others expected him eventually to become. He gives the impression of being unambitious and slow. Living is dreary and offers him no interest or challenge. Because of his reluctance to participate in most aspects of life, he does not grow emotionally or intellectually. In spite of this restricted existence, he is frequently capable of functioning in a sheltered environment, although not in a confident or creative manner. He may experience trouble with school or work and express the desire to stay away from things that should seem exciting and attractive.

In simple schizophrenia, there are no delusions, hallucinations, or indications of illogical thinking. On the contrary, it seems as if the patient prefers not to think. He strives to use his mind as little as possible. He will not try to think abstractly but will prefer to limit his conversation to a few favorite and noncomplex topics.

Although the simple schizophrenic does not show the obvious irregularities of the other types, his mental condition is not up to par for normal living. If he exists in a normal environment in which participation and initiative are expected, his behavior reveals itself to be inappropriate and unsuitable for the demands of everyday life. Although generally not violent or given to grossly disturbed behavior, the simple schizophrenic is a burden to his family. If he has no family, he runs the risk of 'dropping out' or being used by certain exploitative sectors of society. Unless he is successfully treated, it is unlikely that a simple schizophrenic will regain his joy in living and experience personal and spiritual growth.

The Schizoaffective Type

In some patients, in addition to the symptoms that have been described, there are striking shifts in mood that are more characteristic of another condition called *manic-depressive psychosis*. These patients appear depressed at times, happy at other times, even euphoric. The schizoaffective type recovers quickly, more so than the other types, but the attacks tend to recur.

The Course of Schizophrenia

A striking characteristic of schizophrenia is the great variability of its course. Some patients recover from an acute attack in a few hours, days, or months. As we noted, twenty-four-hour and forty-eight-hour schizophrenia have been described.

There is a tendency now in America to follow the procedure adopted in certain other countries whereby a patient's condition would not be considered schizophrenia if, although presenting schizophrenic symptoms, the patient recovers within six months. In French-speaking countries an acute paranoid attack is called not schizophrenia but *bouffée délirante* ('delusional attack'). This way of diagnosing, which is based on the duration of the illness, does not seem to me scientifically valid. An illness that has a brief course resembles the early stage of other cases in which the illness is of longer duration.

Some patients remain sick for a long time, and some (fewer now than before) for the rest of their lives. Some undergo a cyclical course characterized by episodes recurring in a fundamentally vulnerable personality.

The course of a schizophrenic illness that is not arrested and reaches the stage of a very advanced regression can be divided into four stages. Let us remember, however, that most patients seen by psychiatrists in private practice belong in the initial stage. Even if patients eventually undergo a second or third attack, they are generally still in the first stage, because modern types of treatment prevent them from progressing further. This first stage extends from the time the patient starts to lose contact with reality to the full formation of the characteristic symptoms that we have so far described.

In patients who do not recover, the illness may proceed to the second, third, or fourth stages. The second, or advanced, stage is characterized by an apparent acceptance of the illness. The symptoms do not seem to bother the patient as much as before. Life has become more and more restricted and lacks spontaneity. In the third, or preterminal, stage many symptoms have decreased their original intensity, and, because all the types of schizophrenia resemble one another so closely, it is often difficult to distinguish a paranoid from a catatonic. In the fourth stage the behavior is impulsive and reflexlike. It is not important for the reader of this book to know details of the second, third, and fourth stages. In a section of Chapter 9 we shall return to a discussion of patients who have proceeded beyond the first stage.

4. Glimpses into the Schizophrenic World

A description of schizophrenia, as offered in the previous chapter, is useful, but it is not enough. We want to understand better the psychological mechanisms that make the patient interpret life, people, himself, his past, and his future in a different way, different not only from the way other people feel and think, but also from the way he felt and thought before he became ill. He seems a different person; yet he is the same person, and the way he is now has a great deal to do with the way he was before.

In this chapter we cannot take into consideration all the major aspects of the world of the schizophrenic, but we shall select a few important visions of that world that will permit us to obtain a fairly adequate idea of what is happening inside of him.

It does not lead us very far to say that the patient is irrational, illogical, incoherent, unrealistic, inconsistent, bizarre, peculiar. Such characterization is not only superficial, but in some respects inaccurate. Even the mental patient is logical or has a logic of his own. It is true that we see the schizophrenic as an illogical human being, at least when he speaks about his symptoms, and to some extent we are justified in considering him as such, but let us see why we experience him as illogical. In what way are the illogical symptoms of the schizophrenic different from those of other psychiatric patients; for instance, the neurotic? Before proceeding, it may be useful to stress again that understanding the psychological mechanisms of mental patients does not imply knowledge of the cause or the complex causes of the symptoms.

A neurotic patient who is phobic may be afraid to cross streets. He may be terribly afraid of animals. Every time he sees a dog or a cat, he may go into a state of panic. Another neurotic patient who is obsessive-compulsive may have an uncontrollable need to look at the license plate of every passing car and try to memorize the numbers. Another may have the obsession-compulsion that unless he washes his hands five times at each meal, his children are going to become sick and die. All these neurotic patients have retained normal mental functions that enable them to recognize the unreal nature of their symptoms and the absurd demands that these symptoms make on them. They would like very much to lose their symptoms. Nothing would please them more. But they cannot.

On the other hand, a deluded patient who thinks she is the queen of England accepts the symptom; she does not see anything unnatural in it. The idea is accepted as an indisputable truth in spite of what seems to the rest of the world to be the most contradictory evidence. Instead of living in London, the patient lives in Brooklyn; instead of speaking with a British accent, she speaks with a New York accent. Nobody refers to her as 'Your Majesty'; everybody insists on calling her 'Miss Smith.' And yet she repeatedly refers to herself as 'Her Majesty, the queen of England.' We must investigate what change has occurred in the cognitive functions of people like Miss Smith to make them unable to test reality; that is, to distinguish between their fantasy and reality. All of us can have fantasies, daydreams of being Queen Elizabeth, Madame Curie, Albert Einstein, but we know that we are not; we are only daydreaming. Some of us would like to be in the position of Queen Elizabeth; we would like to be as capable and creative as a Madame Curie or an Albert Einstein, but we know that we are not. The mechanisms of schizophrenic thinking, similar to those that make Miss Smith believe that she is the queen of England, have been the object of much investigation from the time of Bleuler, the psychiatrist who, we learned in the previous chapter, coined the term schizophrenia. Before entering into this complex subject, it may be useful to investigate simpler aspects of this abnormal way of thinking.

First of all, we must stress that even the sickest schizophrenic does not always think in a schizophrenic way but does so only when his psychological difficulties compel him to abandon his normal ways of thinking. Moreover, schizophrenics have other mechanisms that, although somewhat abnormal, are used by neurotics and even by normal persons. Let us start with the examination of one of these forms of thinking that is shared by the schizophrenic, the neurotic, and the normal person: *rationalization*. Rationalization is an attempt to provide a logical justification for actions or ideas that are not justifiable but are nevertheless imposed by strong emotional needs. This attempt is made by resorting to explanations that, although not recognized as valid when subjected to careful examination, seem correct and plausible because as explanations they succeed in hiding the illogical content and the real motivation.

Let us examine the rationalization of a normal person. A professional man who planned to attend a lecture did not realize that on that evening he would prefer to remain at home with his family and relax. He looked out of the window, saw that it was raining, and said, 'The weather is bad. It is wiser to stay home.' In this way, the weather became responsible for his not attending the lecture. Let us examine now the rationalization of a schizophrenic patient who was approaching an advanced stage of her illness. She had been born and raised in a South American country in a well-to-do family and had come to the United States in her early twenties after completing her college education. While in the United States she married an American citizen, with whom she had a child. When I first saw her, she was in her middle thirties, had been sick for several years, and showed signs of regression. She appeared somewhat detached, except when she was talking about her husband, for whom she nourished bitter resentment. She would repeatedly say that her husband was a bad man and that she had always known it. When she was asked why she had married her husband if she knew he was such a bad man, she replied, 'The wedding ceremony took place in this country. When the priest asked me if I wanted to marry my husband, he spoke in English and I did not understand him. I said, "I do." '

The rationalization would be facetious if it were not also a revelation of the patient's sorrow. It would be logical if it were not based on illogical premises. The patient obviously understood the question at the wedding ceremony and replied 'I do' in English.

Moreover, she spoke English fairly well at the time of her wedding. Her rationalization, however, cannot be interpreted just at face value as an attempt to justify herself or to disavow her responsibility or to make her marriage illegal. There was much more than that in this apparently absurd rationalization.

The years spent in the United States had a flavor of unreality for her, or at least they seemed to have been lived in an atmosphere of fogginess and confusion. These years were characterized by a series of unfortunate events that culminated in her unhappy marriage. Only her life prior to her coming to the United States – that is, that period of her life when she was speaking Spanish – made sense to her. In her mind what was confused, vaguely motivated, or directly or indirectly connected with pain and sorrow became associated with the English language. We could say that some parts of the patient's life were lived as if symbols and metaphors were reality. The uncertainty and confusion of her North American life came to be seen by her as a linguistic difficulty. Again this symptom, a rationalization, cannot be interpreted just as a technical device to avoid responsibility. It is also and predominantly an expression of her whole life history, of her very personal sorrow, of the difference between the peace (or apparent peace) of her early life and the turbulence (or apparent turbulence) of her married life.

In a way comparable to the work of the fine artist and the poet, a little episode or a single symptom like a rationalization is made to become representative of a much larger segment of reality, of the way a woman has experienced a large part of her married life. But let us examine again the example of rationalization by the normal professional man. That rationalization, too, cannot be taken literally. For him, the bad weather, the storm, his going out at night may be symbolic of the hard, professional, competitive world where he always has to keep abreast, where he has challenges to meet. Staying at home is being protected, being with one's wife, or with mother, or in mother's womb – whatever level of interpretation is more suitable to the specific circumstance. The rationalization of the professional man shows us the dilemma between two types of life he faces and represents the choice between them that he must make at times.

Through careful examination, however, we recognize the difference between the two rationalizations. That of the professional man could stand on its own merit. People at times do stay home because of bad weather. In this case there is a concordance between the obvious, although superficial, reality of the bad weather and the psychodynamic reality of the harsh professional world that is suppressed. That is, the professional man can stay at home for both reasons, because of the weather and because he does not want to meet the challenge of the professional life.

In the rationalization of the South American woman there was no congruence or concordance between the external or superficial reality and the one based on deep psychological problems. The rationalization becomes plausible only if we understand what has been relegated to the depth of the psyche and has been replaced or symbolized by a linguistic difficulty.

From the examples given, and from others that will be reported later in this chapter, it will become evident that a person, even when schizophrenic, almost always attempts to maintain plausibility. Contrary to what is believed by some, few human beings can accept anything that seems irrational to them. The need for rationality is as powerful as the need to gratify the irrational motivation. This need for rationality is always underestimated by people who see the human being as totally dominated, directly or indirectly, by instinctual drives. If the concept *instinct* is to be retained in reference to humans, the instinct towards rationality (including reason and rationalization) must also be acknowledged.

If the need for rationality is never completely abandoned, however, the usual type of rationality is often suspended, especially in situations of severe anxiety or emergency. This will be true to a greater extent in the mental processes that we shall discuss in this chapter. However – and here we cannot avoid marveling at the multiform aspects of the human psyche – every irrationality has its own rationality, that is, its own purpose and mental organization. What appears to us as an illogical element is part of a psychological whole, which can be understood once we know the deep motivation of the patient and the special mental mechanisms that he adopts.

Special Schizophrenic Ways of Thinking

It is not necessary for a person who is not a psychiatrist to know all the rules and the special laws of logic that the schizophrenic uses in support of his complexes or ideas, which to us seem delusional. It is important, however, to keep in mind that when a statement or a belief that seems absurd to us is expressed with great sincerity and even defended by the patient, it is not done out of stubbornness, caprice, antagonism, obstructiveness or simply because the patient wants to be irrational or difficult. To him, his idea is rational, unquestionable, based on an absolute conviction of his truth. His unconscious motivation, a desire that cannot be controlled or from which he cannot escape, obliges the patient to use unusual ways of thinking.

An example that I often use, because it illustrates the phenomenon clearly, is that of a young female patient who thought she was the Virgin Mary. When she was asked why, she whispered, 'I am a virgin; I am the Virgin Mary.' Understanding this requires understanding two mental mechanisms of the patient's illness, both operating in the total picture. In her deep inner self the patient felt inadequate, worthless. The circumstances of her life had devastated her sense of self, of self-esteem. Her self-image had become horrendous and unacceptable to her. Thus she had the need to be not herself but, in a compensatory way, her ideal of feminine perfection – the person to whom she felt extremely close and for whom she had a sense of spiritual kinship. This person was the Virgin Mary. However, she could not convince herself that she was the Virgin Mary if she continued to use her logic, which would remind her that she was only Nancy and that there was no evidence of her being anyone else.

Her illness made her switch to a primitive form of logic, according to which A becomes B if A has at least one quality of B. A (in this case the patient Nancy) becomes B (the Virgin Mary) because A has a quality in common with B, namely *being virgin*. Once the patient adopts this type of thinking, her wish is supported by her new logic. She firmly believed she was the Virgin Mary.

This primitive type of logic follows not the classic Aristotelian laws of thought, obeyed automatically by the normal mind, but a principle that was formulated by a psychiatrist named Von Domarus. The principle, in a slightly modified form, says that whereas the normal person accepts identity (that is, he concludes that two objects or two persons are the same) only upon the basis of identical subjects (totality of the subject), the person who uses primitive logic accepts identity based upon identical predicates, that is, a common quality or part. Total sameness is not necessary for identity.

Among other examples, a patient quoted by Bleuler thought he was Switzerland. How can one explain such a bizarre thought? How can a person be a country? Even in Bleuler's time, Switzerland was one of the few free countries in the world, and the patient had selected the name of this country for the concept of freedom with which he had the impelling need to identify himself. 'Switzerland loves freedom. I love freedom. I am Switzerland.'

A red-haired woman, during an acute schizophrenic episode that followed childbirth, developed an infection in one of her fingers, which became swollen and red. She told the therapist, 'This finger is me.' Pointing to the finger, she said, 'This is my red and rotten head.' She did not mean that her infected finger was a representation of herself but that, in a way incomprehensible to us, it was really herself or an actual duplicate of herself.

Another patient believed that the two men she loved were actually the same person, although one lived in Mexico City and the other in New York. In fact, both played the guitar and both loved her. By resorting to a way of thinking that followed the principle of Von Domarus, she could reaffirm the unity of the image of the man she wanted to love.

Slightly different is the example of a new patient who, while waiting for the first time in my outer office, saw in a magazine an advertisement with a picture of a nude baby. He remembered that he, too, when he was a small child, had been photographed in that way, and 'the bastard,' his father, had not too long ago threatened to show that picture to the patient's girl friend. His seeing that picture in my waiting room, the patient thought, was not an accidental coincidence. He presented the phenomenon commonly found in schizophrenics of seeing nonaccidental coincidences everywhere. The terrible coincidences for which there was no explanation were pursuing him relentlessly.

The phenomenon of coincidences is also related to the principle of Von Domarus. A coincidence is a similar element or event occurring in two or more instances at the same time or on presumedly significant occasions in the life of the patient. The patient, trying to find glimpses of regularities in the midst of the confusion in which he lives, tends to register identical segments of experience and to build systems of regularity upon such identical segments. These systems of supposed regularity support his complexes and his delusions.

Often emphasis on similarity gives rise to unpredictable types of delusional thinking. For instance, a patient had some difficulty at work just prior to his developing a schizophrenic episode. During this episode he believed that many people in the street looked exactly like those who worked in the firm where he was employed. He felt that his co-workers must have many brothers and sisters or even identical twins who were there to disturb him with their presence. He saw a young man who looked like a girl he used to go out with. He immediately thought that this man must be the girl's brother, although he knew that she had no brother. When the patient had improved, he still reported to the therapist his strong tendency to associate people and things with others because of some similarities. However, he was then able to resist the tendency to make abnormal identifications. Any person who has a characteristic in common with an alleged persecutor, like having a beard or red hair or wearing a special dress, may become the persecutor, or a relative of the persecutor, or somehow associated with the persecutor. From these examples it is easy to recognize that many patients at this stage indulge in what has been called an 'orgy of identifications.'

The mechanisms or successive steps of primitive thinking are not known to the schizophrenic, who automatically thinks in this way, just as the normal person automatically applies the Aristotelian laws of logic without even knowing them, or as Molière's character

M. Jourdain always spoke prose without knowing what prose was. For instance, a female schizophrenic patient thinks, without knowing why, that the doctor in charge of the ward is her father and that the other patients are her sisters. A common predicate, a man in authority, leads to the identity between her father and the physician. Another common predicate, that the females in the ward are in the same position of dependency, leads the patient to consider herself and the other inmates as sisters. Of course, these identifications were facilitated by her family situation, ruled by an authoritarian male chauvinist father.

At times, the interpretation of this type of thinking requires more elaboration. For instance, a patient reported by Von Domarus thought that Jesus, cigar boxes, and sex were identical. Study of this delusion disclosed that the common predicate that led to this identification was the state of being encircled. According to the patient, the head of Jesus is encircled by a halo, the package of cigars by the tax band, and the woman by the sexual glance of the man.

The mental processes that I have described in the delusional thinking of the schizophrenic are similar to those reported by Freud in dreams of normal people. The whole field of Freudian symbolism as it appears in dreams, from the point of view of formal structure, is based on Von Domarus's principle. A symbol of X is something that stands for X but also something that retains some similarity with X – a common predicate or characteristic. In a dream, a snake or a fountain pen may symbolize a penis because of the similarity of the elongated shapes. A king may symbolize father and a queen may symbolize mother because of the position of power they enjoy in the family. A box may symbolize a vagina because both a box and a vagina are able to contain something in their cavities. The wife of a dreamer appeared in a dream as having the physical appearance of the dreamer's boss. The two persons were identified in the dream because the dreamer was concerned with a predicate common to both of them (their domineering attitude). The boss was selected as a symbol because in the framework of the dreamer's own special psychology, it was more acceptable to him to be dominated by his boss than by his wife.

We see thus that when a dreamer dreams or a schizophrenic

experiences delusions, they both think in a way that becomes understandable to us as allegory or metaphor. The schizophrenic, when involved in his delusions, seems to live in a metaphorical world. We must remember, however, that this world is metaphorical only for us, not the patient, who accepts it as reality. Carl Jung, the great Swiss psychoanalyst, who later diverged from Freud, said very aptly that if a dreamer acted and thought in his waking life as he does in his dreams he would be a schizophrenic.

Language in Schizophrenia

Language and its relationship to thought disorders is very revealing in schizophrenia. This is a vast subject, and only a few points that may interest the reader will be discussed here.*

In the most pronounced cases, schizophrenic language appears obscure or utterly incomprehensible. Some authors go to the extent of interpreting the lack of clarity of schizophrenic language as an effort on the part of the patient to hide from others, or more probably from himself, the anxiety-provoking content of what he has to say. He does not want to communicate. These authors see in the schizophrenic speech the same mechanism that Freud saw in dreams: an attempt to hide the manifest content. Although this may be the case in some circumstances, the phenomenon of linguistic alterations in schizophrenia has other ramifications, is susceptible to other interpretations, and must also be approached from the point of view of logic and of thinking disorders.

In normal language any word can be considered from three points of view. Let us take, for instance, the world *table*. Table is a concept that means *article of furniture with flat horizontal top set on legs*. We could say that this is the definition of table. In logic this is called the *connotation* of the word table. But table is not just a concept; it may be the object that is meant, that is the table as a physical entity, the table I eat my meals on. In logic this is called the *denotation* of the word table. But table is also a sound, a phonetic entity, a special noise to which a meaning has been attached. This is the *verbalization*. In schizophrenia a frequent

* For a more comprehensive discussion of this topic, see S. Arieti, *Interpretation of Schizophrenia*, 2nd ed. (New York: Basic Books, 1974), Chapter 16.

mental alteration makes the patient give very little importance to the connotation. He concentrates instead on the verbalization, on the word as a sound, a phonetic entity. After this concentration on the verbalization occurs, other mental processes that are stimulated only by the verbalization follow. Consequently, as some examples will reveal, the patient at times seems very obscure and incomprehensible, or almost so, and at other times humorous, as if he wanted to tell us jokes. But what appears as a joke to us is said in all seriousness by the patient.

During a test a patient was asked to explain what life is. She replied, 'I have to know what life you are referring to – *Life* magazine or the sweetheart who can make another individual happy and gay.' A patient who I examined during World War II told me the next time the Japanese attacked the Americans it would be at Diamond Harbor or Gold Harbor. When asked why, she replied, 'The first time they attacked at Pearl Harbor. Next time they will attack at Diamond Harbor or Sapphire Harbor.' She gave the usual literal connotation to the word *pearl*, and this led her to make associations with precious stones.

Often the verbalization is exploited to fit special preoccupations or delusions of the patients. For instance, every time a patient heard the words *home* and *fair*, he thought they were the slang words for homosexual, *homo* and *fairy*. He was preoccupied with the problem of sexual identification and believed that people were subtly referring to his alleged homosexuality. The similarity between these words would not have been noticed or seized upon had the patient not been so preoccupied.

Another patient heard some employees in her office saying that 'Attention should be paid to O. B.' She immediately thought they were referring to her: *O. B.* would stand for *old bag* or for *obstetrics*, thus implying or unfairly accusing her of being pregnant. She had repressed the fact, well known to her, that in the firm there was an order and billing department and that the initials *O.* and *B.* had always been used to refer to the work of that department.

Another patient felt that when people used the word *candies* they were referring to her former boyfriend. She was on a diet and had given up eating candies, just as she had previously given up her boyfriend. The predicate of having given up led the patient to identify candies and boyfriend and to assume that other people would make a similar identification.

When the illness advances, the thought and language disorders become much more pronounced and what the patient says or writes may appear almost or completely incomprehensible. Ideas do not associate as they normally do. What results has been called *word-salad..*

Bleuler wrote that the disease 'interrupts, quite haphazardly, single threads, sometimes a whole group, and sometimes even large segments of the thousands of associative threads which guide our thinking.' According to Bleuler, 'the most important determinant . . . is completely lacking – the concept of purpose.'

We have made much progress in understanding schizophrenic language and thinking since Bleuler wrote those words, partially because Bleuler himself, with his pioneer work, stimulated much research on this topic. Although we still feel that Bleuler gave an accurate description of schizophrenic language and thought, we can no longer share his view that the concept of purpose is lacking. The purpose *is* there, but it may be difficult to find.

It is not necessary for the reader to know the methodology by which difficult speech and writing of schizophrenics are interpreted. However, two examples will be given here to show how a sense of purpose can be recaptured, even if it is conveyed in unusual ways and almost concealed in strange expressions.

We could at first be impressed by the extent of mental disintegration shown in the following passage from a letter by Margaret, a schizophrenic patient.

Dear Dr Arieti,
It Is Because I Am So Passionate That They Brought Me Here.
Doctor Webster Asked Me Why I Was Brought Here And I Couldn't Answer Without A Certain Hesitation, But Now I know, I Know Now:
I'm Too Passionate!
That's Why I Can't Get A Job.
You Had The Wrong Diagnosis.
Take This For Instance.
Look Up The Word Passions In The Encyclopedia (A Masterpiece Of A

Word) And In The Dictionaries. Don't Get Cerebral Meningitis In Your Studies.

But You Will Find That There Is A Difference Between The Passions Of Jesus Of Bethlehem And The Passions Of Blue Beard.

Between The Passion Of Misplaced Sympathies And The Passions Of Suicidal Thoughts.

Are You Passionately In Sympathy With Your Great Poet Dante, Doctor Arieti?

And I Am In Passionate Admiration Of The Works Of Molière, The French Troubadour.

And There Is The Passion Flower.

And The Passion Plays Of Oberammergau.

The patient wants to convey the idea that she was hospitalized because she was too passionate, not because she is mentally ill. She feels a wrong diagnosis was made. Soon, however, Margaret becomes involved with the meaning of the word *passion* and loses the main point. There is no longer logical or directed thinking, and therefore no apparent purpose. Margaret's letter, however, has a meaning. She wants to assert strongly that a wrong diagnosis has been made and that she is not mentally ill. At the time Margaret wrote this letter, she was in a state of fairly advanced regression. She had been hospitalized for a few years and gave the impression of being apathetic or at least emotionally shallow. She did not appear so in her writings, which had a strong emotional impact. Her trouble, she states vehemently, is not mental illness but being 'too passionate.' In her letter, the direction of her thinking soon becomes deflected and focuses on the meaning of *passionate*, in her opinion so difficult a word that the study of it may harm one's nervous system (she warns: Don't develop cerebral meningitis over the study of this word). In everyday language, the words *passion* and *passionate* refer to strong sexual desire, and inability to control such desire could be considered the origin of the patient's trouble. But the patient went beyond this common meaning: Sex was extended to the whole realm of passions, that is, of strong emotions. The word *passion* itself becomes 'a masterpiece.' The patient lists the sublime passion of Jesus Christ as well as the criminal passion of Bluebeard, the pain that comes from having invested affections in the wrong place and that which comes from suicidal thoughts.

She also lists as passion the emotion which comes from the beautiful experience of poetry and art.

Thus a second examination of this letter shows that Margaret is subliminally and subconsciously aware of many things. At best her knowledge reaches an unclear form of consciousness. The extent of her feelings and the range of her intellect, as well as the results of experiences before and during the illness ('misplaced sympathies, suicidal thoughts'), come through in spite of her present psychological disintegration. The meaning is conveyed not by logical progression of thought but by the totality of the thoughts. No matter how disconnected, the letter conveys a tone, an atmosphere, what at times is called a *sphere of meaning*.

In some cases the expressions and writings of schizophrenics consist of word-salad and stereotypes, that is, repetition of the same words in a way that conveys severe impoverishment of thought and loss of meaning. In other cases, however, even when the most pronounced forms of stereotyping and impoverished language are found, it is possible to trace some diffuse, global, or spheric meaning. Let us take as an example the following writing of a very regressed schizophrenic:

> Do I see cake Do I do the reverse of acting
> Yes Do I feel sensually deceived
> thoughts in mental suggestion in increase of
> senses in suggestion
>   senses deceptive
>   in in deception deception deception
>   deception
> vanilla lemon as lemon vanilla as the beginning
> of in in suggestion suggestion suggestion
> suggestion of the suggestions as the
> beginning of in suggestion
> lemon vanilla as inceptibility of the
> reason as lemon as in in suggestion
> suggestion suggestion suggestion of
> the suggestions
>   insuggestion
>   iv
> Do I seeI do in sugget

This is a typical example of word-salad and stereotypes. The first impression we get upon reading it is that it is utter nonsense. We are also impressed by the repetition of some words. Let us try, at least, to grasp the spheric meaning.

The patient is preoccupied with a phenomenon that he cannot understand: Are his senses reliable, or does he undergo mental suggestion? The world he is experiencing is chaotic, fragmentary, uncertain. Almost all the things he observes lead him to two alternative conclusions or symbols that have become prominent to the point of embracing everything else: sense deception or mental suggestion. In other words, is he the victim of his own senses, which deceive him, or is he undergoing mental suggestion, coming either from himself or from the external world? Almost everything comes to be perceived in terms of these two stereotyped concepts: deception and suggestion. He undergoes strange phenomena. 'Do I do the reverse of acting?' That is, 'Do I do the opposite of what I would like to do?' However, a few things remain like islands of reality that are not yet submerged by the invading ocean of deception and suggestibility. 'Do I see cake?' he asks himself; that is, something tangible, concrete. And later he sees lemon and vanilla, colorful and pleasant objects that stand out in the sea of confusion expressed by abstract words. Mental suggestion seems to win out over sense deception. The patient seems to recognize that the trouble is suggestion, and, as a matter of fact, the repetition of the word suggestion has a suggestive quality.

Hallucinations

Hallucinations are important and characteristic symptoms of schizophrenia. They occur in many but not in all cases.

An hallucination is the perception of an external stimulus when no stimulus is present. For instance, a patient hears voices talking to him, or accusing him, but there is nobody there to talk to him. He sees persons who are not there; he may smell an odor which nobody else smells, or taste something which is not there. The most common hallucinations in schizophrenia are auditory: 'the voices.' What the patient allegedly perceives is actually elicited by an internal stimulus; it comes from the individual himself. But inasmuch as the patient believes that he is experiencing something in the external world, the perception is false. Several examples of hallucinations were given in Chapter 3.

There are many ways in which hallucinations are experienced. However, in the typical case we may distinguish three phases. The first consists of the very first time the patient experiences an hallucination. In some cases he may give little importance to the phenomenon, but in others he undergoes a sudden, profound, and staggering experience. He hears a powerful voice or sound with a message directed to him only, a message that is related to his whole psychological being. In many cases it is the response of the patient to this first experience that determines the course of the illness. Although deeply affected and badly frightened, the patient may say to himself, 'What I hear is not true; it is only my imagination.' If he is able to respond in that way, he still has the power to resist schizophrenia. Unfortunately, in the majority of cases the patient, because of previous psychological conditions, is more indignant than frightened, and more disposed to accept the external reality of the experience. Instead of thinking, 'This is not a real voice,' he says to himself, 'The voice is real, but what it says is false.' In quite a few cases the patient continues to think in a way that will lead him even further from reality. Often he thinks, 'What does it mean that I hear this voice? Why does it say these things about me?' and concludes, 'I am accused. I am persecuted. They talk behind my back in a disparaging, insulting manner.'

After this early experience the patient proceeds to a second phase during which he expects to have hallucinations, and indeed he has them. The third phase occurs only in patients who reach an advanced stage of the illness. Hallucinations have become such a familiar phenomenon and their occurrence so frequent that the patient accepts them as an important part of his life.

It is not necessary for the reader to know all the theories advanced to explain hallucinations. Perhaps the most important thing to remember is that hallucinations are thoughts of the patient that have undergone a transformation and consequently reflect what the patient feels about himself and the relationships between himself, other persons, and the world in general. The transformation consists in these thoughts having become perceptions, audible (or visible) to the patient. At times there are intermediary stages: The patient hears his own thoughts and believes other people, too, can hear them.

It may be useful to show the similarities between dreams and hallucinations. Dreams, too, are ideas and feelings of the dreamer translated into hallucinations. While in schizophrenia the hallucinations are predominantly auditory, in dreams they are visual. The dreamer too, while he dreams, believes in the reality of his dream, just as the schizophrenic believes in the external reality of his experiences. Only when the dreamer is about to wake up does he realize that his dream is a dream. Similarly, the patient realizes that his hallucinations and other symptoms were imaginary when he starts to recover from his illness.

During the illness the patient, unless properly treated, cannot realize that hallucinations are deceptive. Until recently it was thought that hallucinations could not be corrected. They would disappear by themselves when the patient recovered or was treated with drug therapy. Actually, a successful method has been devised recently to treat hallucinations with purely psychotherapeutic methods.*

* See S. Arieti, *Interpretation of Schizophrenia*, 2nd ed. (New York: Basic Books, 1974), Chapter 37, pp. 573-76.

5. Causes

We often hear that psychiatrists disagree about the causes of the conditions they are treating. The statement is correct, but it should not be taken as an indication of confusion or a motive for discouragement. It has other implications, prominent among them the fact that most psychiatrists want to avoid the mistake of *reductionism* – that is, of reducing to a small cause or a simple formula what they sense to be a complicated problem with many dimensions.

The disagreement in psychiatry is no greater than in several other branches of medicine. There are many common physical illnesses about whose causes we know even less than what we know about psychiatric conditions. We also must keep in mind that although it would be far preferable to have exact and complete knowledge of the causes of diseases of the organism, effective treatment or amelioration may take place even when our knowledge of causes is incomplete. This has actually been accomplished in recent medical history. For instance, let us take for comparison diabetes, a condition about which we have a great deal of information and that we are able to treat successfully in most cases. We know that diabetes is caused by the inability of the pancreas to produce enough insulin for the requirements of the organism, but why the pancreas does not always function adequately we do not know. We know that diabetes tends to run in some families, but not all members of those families are affected. We know that it tends to occur in people who are overweight, but not all people who are overweight develop diabetes. We know that people ingesting excessive amounts of carbohydrates have a higher incidence of the condition, but not all (or even most) of the people who consume a diet rich in carbohydrates develop it. Finally, although most cases of diabetes are treated successfully, none are cured.

Concerning psychiatric conditions, it is correct to say that at the present stage of knowledge we must consider them to be the result of a *combination* of causes. Probably only when this particular combination occurs does the illness ensue. Perhaps if all the causes (or elements of the combination) are present except one, the illness does not develop. If it is so, it may be sufficient to eliminate – if we can – only one element (or one cause) of the complicated causal set in order to prevent the illness.

The reader who has gone through the first four chapters of this book has already realized that psychiatric illnesses have an identity of their own that distinguishes them from physical diseases. Even when we can speak of multiple causes in reference to diseases of the body, we can say that all of them belong to the same physical world. The causes may be invisible to the naked eye, like bacteria, but they all function through physicochemical actions on the organism. In psychiatric conditions such as schizophrenia, some causes may be directly related to the biological or physicochemical world, but other causes have to be studied at different levels – psychological and sociological – even if their ultimate effect is on the physicochemical world or if their first casual connections with schizophrenia are in the physicochemical world. The interchange between these various domains will be clarified in this chapter.

Although we have stated that most psychiatrists consider psychiatric illnesses to be the result of many factors, there are some psychiatrists who do consider them to be the result of only one cause or who assign almost exclusive importance to one cause. This is important for the family of the patient to know, because the specific cause held responsible for the illness reflects the concept that a given psychiatrist will have about the patient. The converse is also often true in psychiatry. The attitude that a therapist has toward the patient will influence his theoretical position. Does he see before him an organism defective in its metabolism, or a suffering human being, or a person who copes abnormally with the difficulties of life, or all of these? A rule of thumb – by no means valid in all cases – is that therapists who rigidly adhere to a theoretical standpoint also have an inflexible attitude towards the patient, or at least in the administration of treatment.

Concerning schizophrenia, too, we can say that according to many psychiatrists the special combination or causal set that leads to the condition consists of three groups of factors:

1. Biological factors, or physical conditions of the organism, probably inherited.

2. Psychological factors, or conditions developed in childhood or later and having to do with the family and possibly other people.

3. Social factors, or conditions of the environment at large or of the society to which the patient belongs.

Although these factors may start to affect the patient at different times, eventually they interrelate, may act simultaneously, and form what we have referred to as the causal set. Nevertheless, for the sake of clarity we shall discuss them separately. Our exposition will not be complete. We shall take into consideration only the major factors, our aim being not an exhaustive and all-inclusive discussion of this vast topic, but a presentation stressing what is particularly pertinent to readers of this book.

Biological Factors

The belief that schizophrenia has a hereditary basis originated from the frequently made observation that the condition occurs more often in some families than in others. Many statisticians seem to agree that schizophrenia occurs in a little less than 1 percent of the general population, approximately 0.85 percent. On the other hand, in some families that have been examined for three generations the incidence is much higher. If a parent or a sibling is suffering from schizophrenia, the incidence rises to between 4 and 10 percent. On the basis of these simple and direct observations one could assume that schizophrenia has a hereditary basis. The problem, however, is not that simple. There are some diseases, like Huntington's chorea, hemophilia, muscular dystrophy, and retinitis pigmentosa, whose hereditary nature is beyond question.

Geneticists, the people who study how hereditary traits are transmitted from generation to generation, have been able to recognize that these diseases follow Mendelian laws, or derivatives of Mendelian laws. Geneticists, however, have not been able to determine these laws in reference to schizophrenia. A Mendelian law describes a pattern of transmission of hereditary traits as originally defined by Gregor Mendel, a monk who showed that such traits are transmitted through the chance combination of pairs of hereditary units that we now call *genes*. A gene is said to be dominant when it produces an observable effect (for instance, a disease) in the offspring, even though the pair contains a recessive gene. A recessive gene does not produce an observable effect, like a hereditary disease, unless the other gene of the pair is also recessive.

Several combinations of genes result, which explains the variations in transmission of hereditary characteristics and hereditary diseases. It is not important for us to study gene combinations. What is important for us to know is that no combination has been found that could explain the distribution of schizophrenia in a family.

Geneticists have demonstrated that identical twins have exactly the same genetic code. Thus if one of them inherits a hereditary disease, the other also ineluctably inherits it, whether the disease is dominant or recessive. There is no better way to study the transmission of hereditary diseases than by collecting statistics of identical twins. If the illness is a psychiatric illness, the best way is to study twins reared apart, in order to eliminate the influence that the family may have had in rearing the child. Such studies have been done by several researchers, the most recent having been carried out by Scandinavian authors. They found that if one identical twin has suffered from schizophrenia, the other will suffer from schizophrenia at some time in his life in about 35 percent of cases, even if the twins are reared apart. Thus the incidence of the illness is approximately forty times greater than one would expect in the general population. This finding is certainly impressive, but even more impressive is the fact that in 60 percent of pairs of identical twins reared apart, one twin is *not* suffering and is *not* going to suffer from schizophrenia.

Since identical twins are genetically equivalent, differences between them must be the result of factors that are not hereditary in nature. And the difference or discordance in relation to schizophrenia in identical twins is greater than the concordance. If schizophrenia were a purely genetic condition, the concordance would have to be 100 percent. It is thus fair to assume that whatever the genetic factors operating in schizophrenia are, they provide only a potential (or biological predisposition) for the illness; other factors are necessary to convert this potential into an actual disease. If genes carry this predisposition, these genes must be activated by other factors, possibly later in the development of the individual.

Long ago many researchers tried to find this biological predisposition or substratum for the disease in some abnormalities of the brain. When the science of neuropathology developed, many researchers tried to find histological alterations in the brain of the schizophrenic, but all researches proved unfruitful. Even under the most powerful microscope it is impossible to distinguish the brain cells of a schizophrenic from those of a normal person. Also, the relatively recent field of electron microscopy has not yet contributed in a positive way to finding a cellular pathology of schizophrenia.

Recently biochemical studies of the central nervous system have appeared to be much more promising. Many investigators thought that the hereditary predisposition may be transmitted through some changes in the biochemical activities of the nervous system. Even some authors who do not believe that a schizophrenic predisposition is inherited think that the schizophrenic process is ultimately a biochemical process, no matter what the original cause of the illness was.

There is some evidence in support of this hypothesis. First of all, theories of the physiology of the nervous system have undergone a drastic change in the last twenty years or so. Whereas before it was believed that transmission of messages between nerve cells (neurons) was accomplished by electric current at the terminal portions (synapses), now the mode of transmission has been demonstrated to be biochemical.

Other evidence – that is, however, quite debatable – is the positive effect of drug therapy. Many people think that if a chemical product (a drug like a phenothiazine, for instance) produces a beneficial effect, the condition that is treated must also have a chemical foundation. This type of reasoning does not yield to absolute proof. First, the improvement is only symptomatic. In other words, although the symptoms of the illness disappear, the cause is not eliminated and the condition may reappear, as we shall see in Chapter 6. Second, even a psychological condition can be improved by a chemical substance. Let us take an example from daily life. A forty-year-old woman has a serious argument with her husband that reveals to her once more the severe marital difficulties she has to contend with. She is anxious and unhappy, and does not know what to do. She is reluctant to seek help in the form of marital counseling or marital therapy. She decides to take 5 milligrams of Valium (diazepam) and the anxiety and sadness soon disappear. While she is under the influence of the pill, she does not feel overwhelmed by her marital problems.

It is obvious in this case that the origin of this woman's trouble is psychological. It is also obvious that a chemical substance has removed the conscious effects of her difficulties. Her husband may have taken a similar course of action, or he may have done what people used to do more frequently when pills like Valium did not exist – gone to a bar and had a few drinks. He, too, has drowned his sorrow in a chemical substance. Similarly, the fact that schizophrenic symptoms are relieved by biochemical methods is not conclusive proof that schizophrenia is totally biological or biochemical in nature. A predisposition to react with great despondency to a marital problem, like our forty-year-old woman did, may also be partially biological in nature. In fact, not all persons in similar circumstances are overwhelmed to such an extent and need the relief of Valium or similar products. Not all those with similar problems need to drown their sorrows in alcohol.

Many researchers think that they have found definite biochemical alterations in schizophrenics. Here the same question arises. Even if these biochemical alterations are confirmed, are they the cause of schizophrenia or its effect? It is obvious that whatever occurs in the brain has a biochemical counterpart. It is also possible that a vicious circle develops. Psychological problems may bring about biochemical alterations that in their turn produce an alteration of psychological functions. It could also be that original biological alterations bring about psychological dysfunctions that then bring about additional biological alterations. Many authors believe that they have found evidence that a biochemical alteration exists in schizophrenia. We shall not discuss the theories that have proved unfounded, but we shall consider those researches that still seem promising.

One of them is based on the transmethylation hypothesis. In 1959 it was discovered that in the normal brain, a biochemical process called the *transmethylation* of norepinephrine to epinephrine occurs. Many authors have advanced the hypothesis that an abnormal change in this process occurs in schizophrenia and have shown results proving it. This alteration would disrupt the delicate balance between the sympathetic nervous system (which operates mainly through the norepinephrine) and the parasympathetic nervous system (which operates mainly through a substance called *acetylcholine*). Other authors believe that schizophrenia may be brought about by a deficiency in the brain of a substance called *serotin*.

Seymour S. Kety, who has probably made the most extensive studies in the United States of the biochemistry of schizophrenia, has concluded that no certain evidence of a definite metabolic disorder has been demonstrated.

Four verifications would be necessary to prove that a given chemical substance produces schizophrenia:

1. The chemical substance must be isolated and be found only in schizophrenics.

2. If found in conditions other than schizophrenia, it must be found in schizophrenic patients in quantities that are significantly different from those of nonschizophrenics.

3. The substance should reproduce the disorder when introduced into nonschizophrenic persons in certain quantities.

4. A greater sensitivity, allergy, or other kind of abnormal

reaction to a special substance should be apparent in schizophrenic patients.

As we have already mentioned, many authors have indeed found biochemical alterations in schizophrenic patients. However, their findings do not satisfy any of the four mentioned requirements. That is not to say, of course, that future research will not lead to more positive results.

Conclusions

A hereditary predisposition to schizophrenia seems to have been ascertained. In itself it is not sufficient to 'cause' schizophrenia. Moreover, no hereditary law of schizophrenia has been discovered. No gene related to schizophrenia has been individualized, biochemically or biophysically. Biochemical changes do occur in schizophrenia, but their origin and significance have not been clarified. We do not even know whether they are a cause, a predisposition, or an effect of the disorder. Anatomically, no change has been found in the central nervous system of schizophrenics.

Psychological Causes

We shall now examine another, completely different category of causes: the psychological. The premise underlying this category is that psychological factors would affect the psyche or the mind of the individual in such an adverse way as to lead eventually to schizophrenia if compensatory factors have not intervened in the meantime.

As I have already mentioned, the acceptance of psychological causes does not rule out a biological predisposition. Many authors, myself included, believe that adverse psychological causes would not in themselves lead to schizophrenia, if a biological predisposition did not exist. Conversely, a biological predisposition is not a sufficient cause of schizophrenia if its effects have not been accrued by a sequence of adverse psychological circumstances. Dr Robert Cancro, who is among the researchers who have done the most accurate recent work on schizophrenia, likes to use the following persuasive metaphor: Just as the sperm and the egg are necessary to produce a fetus, so environmental, psychological, and genetic factors are necessary to bring about schizophrenia.

Childhood and Family Environment

What are these psychological factors? Many authors thought that they would be found in the circumstances of the patient's childhood, in the way his family raised and treated him. Some authors have attributed great importance to the abnormality of the family as a whole; others have focused on the unhappy marriage of the parents or on the personality of the father or on interaction with the siblings. The personality and attitude of the mother remain, in the opinion of many, the most important psychological factor. The future patient would spend his childhood in an environment in which relationships with other people were characterized by intense anxiety or hostility, by detachment, or by a combination of these feelings.

These statements contain a great deal of truth, but they have been exaggerated or expressed in terms that evoke unjustified feelings of guilt in the families of patients, and especially in the mother. Some authors have described mothers of schizophrenics as women deprived of maternal feeling. It is more correct to say that these mothers have at times been overcome by the difficulties of living. The difficulties have become enormous not only because of their unhappy marriages but also, and most of all, because of their neuroses and the neurotic attitudes built up in interacting with their children.

There is another important point to be taken into consideration. Adverse assessments of mothers of schizophrenics were made at a time during which drastic changes in the sociological role of women were in a state of incubation. It was a period that immediately preceded the women's liberation era, a time when a woman had to contend fully but tacitly with her newly recognized need to assert her equality. She could no longer accept submission, yet she strove to fulfill her traditional role. Social factors entered into the intimacy of family life and complicated the parental roles of both mothers and fathers.

It was also a time when the so-called nuclear family, an invention of urban industrial society, came into its full existence. The nuclear family consists of a small number of people who live in little space, compete for room and for material and emotional possessions, and are ridden by hostility and rivalry. The home is often greatly deprived of educational, vocational, and religious values. The nuclear family is destructive not only for the children but also for the parents, and especially for the woman.

I believe that during childhood, and later in life, not only must the future patient sustain the impact of intense negative emotions, such as tension, fear, anxiety, hostility, and detachment – no matter who or what is the original source of such emotions – but he also has to contend with the alterations in his development that are consequent to such exposure, and perhaps with some intrinsic qualities that make him less capable of coping with adverse circumstances.

In summary, it is too easy (and too disastrous in its possible consequences) to jump to the conclusion that the mother of the schizophrenic is responsible for the illness of her child. If some mothers of schizophrenics have not been good mothers, we have to consider this realistic fact in more definite terms: That particular mother could not be a good mother for that particular child in the particular situation in which she found herself. Thus we can recognize three different factors acting concurrently: the mother (or her neurosis); the family, with all its difficulties and troubles; and the child, with his own biological predisposition and sensitivity.

Like the prevailing psychiatric literature, we have stressed the role of the mother, who is usually the parent more involved in the upbringing of the child. However, the father also has to be fully considered – first, because in numerous instances he is actually the parent more involved with a particular child, and second, because he may have an indirect adverse effect on the child through his undesirable attitude toward the patient's mother and other members of the family.

In conclusion, the early environment of the child is certainly important and affects the rest of his whole life, including his proclivity to develop schizophrenia. However, this is only part of the picture. Among the psychological causes of schizophrenia we must include the way the child experienced his environment. An undue sensitivity or a special biological predisposition probably made him react too strongly to some stimuli, especially to unpleasant ones. In addition, we must see how the child's experiences of the environment were assimilated, that is, became parts of his psyche. If the experiences were unduly strong, it is possible that they remained as disturbing components of his psyche and promoters of trouble and unrest. Finally, we must include the ways by which the assimilation affected the subsequent events of the patient's life. His whole life history has to be studied.

Development of Special Types of Personality

When we review the whole life of the patient prior to the appearance of the illness, we may distinguish four periods: The first, early childhood, is lived intensely by the patient, within family situations that he experiences too strongly and incorrectly.

In the second period (late childhood) the patient generally develops, as a reaction to the difficulties of the first period, a special type of personality that, unless corrected, becomes more pronounced in adolescence and later. One of these types of personality is the *schizoid* type, that is, the person who, as a result of early experiences, automatically expects unpleasant relationships with other people and becomes aloof, detached, less emotional than the average person, less concerned, and less involved. Secretly he remains very sensitive, but he has learned to avoid anxiety and anger in two ways: by making himself as inconspicuous as possible, putting physical distance between himself and situations that are apt to arouse these feelings; and by repressing emotions.

The physical distance is maintained by avoiding relationships with other people or refraining from actions that may displease others. The child, and later the adolescent, becomes quiet. He develops the wrong idea that 'doing nothing' means being a good child. He may grow older with a deeply rooted pessimism about the outcome of his actions.

A characteristic of the schizoid person is his difficulty in looking into the eyes of the person with him. The schizoid child, and even more so the schizoid adolescent and young adult, may look elsewhere or make only fleeting eye contact. Eye contact makes him intensely aware not only that another person is there, but also that that person is looking at him. As long as the other person does not look at him, the other may be experienced as a person who does not threaten. As soon as he looks, he becomes an older person, an intruder, perhaps an inquisitor.

Another type of personality that develops in individuals who are psychologically predisposed to become schizophrenic is the *stormy* type. Patients of this type find other people distressing, and they deal with them in different, inconsistent ways – at times by being compliant and accommodating to an excessive degree, at other times by being demanding and aggressive, at still other times by being detached. We cannot predict what type of behavior they will adopt on a given occasion.

Adolescence and Young Adulthood

The third period, which generally starts at puberty, may also be a turbulent phase of life. The adolescent may be bothered by sexual urges, but most of all by an image that he has acquired of himself, an image he cannot accept, as we shall clarify shortly. First, we must stress that the type of personality the patient had previously acquired and that was supposed to be a protection or a defense has become an additional handicap. The schizoid, who detached himself and limited his contacts with life, becomes awkward, clumsy, and less able to deal with daily events and with others. The adolescent with a stormy personality cannot establish an adequate sense of self-identity and is not able to answer certain fundamental questions that he asks himself. Who is he and what do his family, acquaintances, and society at large expect from him? If he ever finds out what others demand from him, will he be able to live up to these expectations? Even more crucial is the question of what he expects of himself.

These questions are not asked in a general, abstract, theoretical, or philosophical sense. Philosophical questions of this kind are normal occurrences in bright adolescents and young adults. The person vulnerable to schizophrenia, and especially the stormy person, is concerned with these problems in a more concrete way and in reference only to his specific relationships with others. When we say that he asks himself these questions, we do not necessarily mean that he literally speaks to himself about them, although that may also happen. Often these questions and the inability to answer them are not expressed in words but are felt, as a sense of drifting aimlessly, of not being able to find oneself.

The schizoid person uses mechanisms suggested by his detachment. He becomes a silent follower, a wallflower, an isolated person. But the stormy person cannot compromise in that way. He is forever searching for his role in the world, although he does not meet with success. He still tries to 'reach' people, although he is hurt every time he tries. He still harbors ambitions, although he becomes increasingly discouraged.

The difficulties increase as the inability of this individual to find his place extends beyond the family circle and involves a larger number of peers, acquaintances, and people in the community in which he lives. What role does he play with them? What do they think of him? When later he enters the working world, the same uncertainty creeps in as an inability to find himself as a member of a certain profession or trade. These feelings are further increased by the competition that he senses all around him. Although feelings of this kind are experienced by neurotics, too, they are much more pronounced in those individuals who have a stormy personality and are vulnerable to schizophrenia.

Stormy personalities often are compliant to the point of extreme submissiveness; at other times they are aggressive and hostile; less often, they withdraw into an ivory tower of complete detachment. When they are not detached, they are very anxious; anxiety rules their lives. They are, therefore, very vulnerable; every little event has the power of unchaining a crisis. The life of these persons in general is a series of crises.

Stormy personalities often live in an atmosphere of catastrophe and doom. Still, they show a great capacity to recuperate and seem able to recover strength, spirits, and good humor easily. Generally, however, they do a poor job of covering up the underlying unrest with this shallow and effervescent attitude. When they are in a relatively good mood, they harbor grandiose fantasies and even paranoid tendencies. They are going to be great and successful if they are just given a chance. They are going to get married to wonderful persons, and so forth. They like extremes only; for them, everything is black or white. Acceptance means devotion and love; nonacceptance means utter rejection and hate. There are no nuances in their lives.

Changes in mood and attitude do not relieve these people. Some of them resort to excessive use of drugs and alcohol. The crises they go through often weaken them progressively and are frequently precipitated by little happenings, magnified by these stormy persons, who unconsciously see in them reproductions of situations that produced anxiety in early childhood. At other times the crises are really precipitated by critical situations that arise as the anxiety of these stormy persons forces them to inappropriate actions (hasty marriages, love affairs, absurd jobs, sudden marital separation and divorce, and so forth). Things do not just happen to them, as they seem to happen to schizoid persons. Stormy people seem to search actively for a meaningful way of living.

Many schizoid or stormy persons never develop schizophrenia. They retain this type of personality during their entire lives unless, of course, timely therapy or unforeseen circumstances direct them toward a different type of adjustment.

Some increase the abnormality of their behavior so that many psychiatrists consider them preschizophrenics, latent schizophrenics, or borderline schizophrenics. Most of them succeed in living a socially permissible, though inadequate, life. However, in many cases the schizoid or stormy character structures eventually fail to constitute adequate protection.

For several reasons, the difficulties become increasingly apparent as the individual proceeds toward adulthood. The school situation, the increasing sexual desires, and the search for a position in a competitive world put a serious strain on his character armor. The defenses that the youngster was able to mobilize earlier in life proved to be fairly efficient when he had to contend exclusively or predominantly with his family. Now he feels he has to deal with the world at large. In spite of his emotional detachment, the schizoid person resents the fact that both family and society demand that he give up his detachment and withdrawal – a request that he cannot fulfill. His schizoid characteristics not only do not protect him but they actually handicap him when social pressures compel him to do things in spite of his withdrawal. He feels 'pushed around.' He does things haphazardly and halfheartedly and cannot exploit his full potentiality. His lack of experience in dealing with people increases his fears. When he succeeds in evading his schizoid attitudes and accomplishing things, the old sensitivity tends to come back and he experiences tremendous anxiety. The world now appears to him to be populated by millions of authorities, ready to criticize him. The competitive spirit of our society, where everybody is supposed to assert himself or show how good he is, makes his predicament worse. Handicapped as he is, he often fails, and no wonder. Any additional failure increases his feeling of inadequacy and predisposes him to subsequent failures.

Progressive maladaptation has many different aspects and courses. At times, although it is very pronounced, it is not noticed by people who are not closely associated with the patient. On the contrary, the lack of emotional involvement and the slow tempo confer on the individual a certain poise that may even be appealing to some who do not recognize the underlying unrest. In other cases an insidious maladaptation leading to schizophrenia may become apparent even to the inexperienced observer, but only in some areas. For instance, the scholastic record may reveal a steady decline. The patient was a good student in grammar school, was less than average in high school, and could not function at all in college.

Starting from adolescence, concern with the sexual aspect of life expands tremendously. In relationship to the psychology of schizophrenia, sexual life is important not in itself but only if meanings attached to it adversely affect the self-image. If the person sees himself as a sexually inadequate person, a homosexual, or an undesirable sexual partner, or as lacking sexual control or having no definite sexual identity, he may develop a devastating concept of himself.

Despair, Panic, Break with Reality

Sooner or later the person who develops schizophrenia reaches the conclusion that the future will not redeem the present or the past. It is when he comes to believe that the future has no hope, that the promise of life will not be fulfilled, and that the future may be even more desolate than the present that the psychological decline characteristic of this third period reaches its culmination. The patient feels threatened from all sides, as if he were in a jungle. It is not a jungle where lions, tigers, snakes, and spiders are to be found, but a jungle of concepts – in this case ideas about himself – where the threat is not to survival but to the self-image. The dangers are concept-feelings such as that of not belonging, being unwanted, unloved, unlovable, inadequate, unacceptable, inferior, awkward, clumsy, peculiar, different, rejected, humiliated, guilty, unable to find his own way among the different paths of life, disgraced, discriminated against, kept at a distance, suspected, and so on. Is this a manmade jungle created by civilization in place of the jungle to which primitive tribes are exposed? The answer lies in the understanding of a circular process.

To a large extent the collectivity of humans, in its historical heritage and present conditions, has made this jungle, but to a large extent the patient, too, has created it. Sensitized as he is, because of past experiences and psychological defenses that have crippled more than protected him, he distorts the environment. At this point his distortion is not yet a paranoid projection or a delusion. It is predominantly experienced as anguish, increased vulnerability, fear, anxiety, mental pain. Now the patient feels not only that he is unacceptable to the segment of the world that is important to him, but also that he will be unacceptable to others as long as he lives. He is excluded from the busy, relentless ways of the world. He does not fit; he is alone. He experiences ultimate loneliness; he becomes unacceptable even to himself. This is the real tragedy: to be unacceptable to oneself. It is at this point that a state of panic occurs.

This particular state of panic is at first experienced as a mixture of something that is very clear (as the devastating self-image) and something that is unclear and gloomy. The obscure forces, generally silent but now reemerging in a tumultuous way, are the experiences of early childhood – unpleasant, not necessarily because the childhood environment really was so unsatisfactory, but because the patient has distorted and magnified the negative aspects of his experiences. During this stage of panic the patient finds himself unable to do anything. Now events seem to happen to him. He is no longer a doer but a passive agent.

The Manifest Illness

At this point the fourth period starts; that is, the illness manifests itself in its obvious, clinical forms. The patient makes a break with reality and withdraws in the drastic way that we have described in other chapters. At other times he starts to project and to express paranoid ideas. During the state of panic, the patient had, so to speak, protected the world from blame and to a large extent had considered himself responsible for his own defeat. Now he again externalizes this feeling. He senses a vague feeling of hostility in the air. The world is terrible. A sensation of threat surrounds him. He cannot escape from it.

At a clinical level the illness starts not only when these ideas and feelings are projected to the external world, but also when they become specific. The vast and indefinite feelings become definite and finite, the imperceptible becomes perceptible, the vague menace is transformed into a specific threat. It is no longer the whole horrible world that is against the patient; *they* are against him. No longer has he a feeling of being under scrutiny, under the eyes of the world; no longer does he harbor a mild sense of suspiciousness toward his unfriendly neighbors. The sense of suspiciousness becomes the conviction that *they* follow, watch, influence, or even control him. The vague, the general, and the abstract are reduced to the specific. *They* are a specific representation of external threats; later *they* are more definitely recognized as FBI agents, neighbors, or other specific persecutors. Whereas during the third period the patient often felt that millions of authorities were justified in having the lowest opinion of him, now he feels that a few malevolent, powerful people are unfair to him and are the cause of his trouble. The patient often experiences some phenomena that convince him that something is being done or ordained against him. He is the victim of a plot. He is accused of being a spy, a murderer, a traitor. He hears hallucinatory voices that repeat these accusations. He is unhappy, fearful, often indignant.

At this point it may be important to discuss certain points already referred to in Chapter 3. One's first impression might be that the development of these symptoms is not a defensive maneuver at all. The patient is indeed suffering. However, a psychodynamic interpretation of schizophrenia views these phenomena differently. If we go a little deeper into the matter, we are able to recognize that the transformation of inner conflicts into symptoms that refer to the external world is advantageous to the patient. As unpleasant as it is to be accused by others, it is not as unpleasant as to accuse oneself, to be unacceptable to oneself.

Because of the new ways of thinking described in Chapter 4, the accusation assumes a specific form. For instance, the externalized feeling of being a failure appears as accusations not of failure but of being a spy or a murderer. These accusations seem worse than the original self-accusations but have the advantage of being easily attributed to others. The patient who believes he is accused feels falsely accused. Thus, although the accusation is painful, it is not injurious to the self-esteem. On the contrary, in comparison to the state he was in before he became ill, the patient often experiences a rise in self-esteem, often accompanied by a feeling of martyrdom. The person who is really accused now is not the patient, but the persecutor who is accused of persecuting the patient. The danger, which used to be an internal one, is now transformed by the illness into an external one. In this transformation actually lies the psychodynamic significance of the most common type of schizophrenia, the paranoid. Guilt feeling is eliminated. In some cases pleasant self-images that the patient previously did not allow himself to entertain are now recaptured and often assume a grandiose, distorted, grotesque appearance.

Conclusions

Psychological events in the life of a patient are very important among the various causes of schizophrenia, even if these events are facilitated by a biological predisposition.

Family situations and experiences of childhood, adolescence, and young adulthood become a chain of causes and effects that eventually lead to a precarious, vulnerable way of living. Throughout his life the vulnerable person tries to build psychological defenses, that is, psychological means by which he tries to protect his self-identity, individuality, and self-esteem. When other defenses prove unsatisfactory and he cannot accept himself at all, he resorts to what can be called a psychotic defense. The symptoms of schizophrenia appear and permit him to survive in a less unhappy way.

Thus the major psychological trends in the life of the schizophrenic can be seen as causes consisting in their turn of many smaller causes, most of which are interconnected.

The Psychosociocultural Causes

We shall present only a brief discussion of psychosociocultural causes because, although they are very important, they are of limited concern to the family of the patient or people who are in close contact with him. Sociocultural factors interest in particular those professionals who want to prevent the occurrence of schizophrenia, but once the illness has already appeared in a particular patient, it is too late to attempt to change the sociocultural environment for his sake. Moreover, these factors can be changed only slowly and require work on a large scale, carried out by sociologists, politicians, educators, epidemiologists, and all the other professionals who study communities and collectivities. For a psychiatrist it is important to stress that in most instances sociocultural factors affect the individual through the intermediary action of psychological processes.

It is known that poverty, deprivation, social stress, immigration, being a member of a minority, and living in slum areas all increase the incidence of the disorder. We must be able to translate these statistical data in terms of human suffering. For instance, we must ascertain whether or not these social factors facilitate mental illness by decreasing among a certain group of people the possibility that they will either become good parents or receive good parental care. It is also important to ascertain whether social factors decrease the self-esteem of the individual and thus facilitate the occurrence of mental illness.

An increased incidence of schizophrenia has been ascertained in big urban centers, and especially in industrial centers. Anything that causes human suffering, decrease in self-esteem, and loss of hope may be an indirect factor. A society that fosters a spirit of competition among its members creates a feeling of low self-esteem in those who come to consider themselves losers and makes them more vulnerable to psychological difficulties. Justice, equal opportunities, and the possibility of living in satisfactory ways all decrease the chance that unfavorable factors will act on the individual.

However, when it comes to schizophrenia, we are often confronted with an opposite set of circumstances. Very undesirable extenuating and taxing external or realistic events not only do not precipitate a schizophrenic illness but at times even seem able to obstruct it. During and immediately after World War II, in some defeated European countries the incidence of schizophrenia decreased. Conditions of obvious danger, as they occur in time of war, national defeat, and adversities that affect the whole community, do not in themselves precipitate schizophrenia. They may cause anxiety and psychological disorders, but they do not necessarily hurt the sense of self. In the state of war or military defeat, a feeling of solidarity or common destiny and the absence of personal responsibility for what is happening may even be helpful to the self-image.

Conclusions

Social factors that produce suffering may indirectly facilitate schizophrenia through the intermediary action of psychological processes, especially when they decrease the likelihood of receiving good parental care and when they adversely affect the individual's self-esteem. If at this point we try again to define schizophrenia in terms that refer to its causes, we must say that at the present stage of our knowledge schizophrenia is believed to be a condition with mixed etiology, in which biological, psychological, and sociocultural factors act together to bring about regressive forms of psychological function and behavior, with the characteristics described in previous chapters.

6. Main Methods of Treatment

To Search for Help

Whether the illness is only predicted, suspected, or already present in its most obvious form, professional help is necessary and has to be found without delay. No matter how generous of time, work, and care the family members are willing to be, they cannot adequately do by themselves all that the situation requires. Fortunately they are not alone. There are a large number of professionals who can intervene promptly and effectively.

The family (or the patient himself) may not know how to obtain professional help or how to find an available doctor who is particularly suitable for that special case. In situations in which the family members are completely at a loss, they may even resort to the telephone book. They must look for the local branch of the National Association for Mental Health or for a community mental health center and make inquiries. They may call a teaching hospital in the community. They may also call the county medical association and obtain a list of properly qualified psychiatrists. Or, they may call the American Psychiatric Association in Washington, D.C., and ask for the names of a few psychiatrists in the area where the patient resides.

A better way, however, is one that relies on a personal contact. The family doctor, a general practitioner, may refer the patient to a psychiatrist in whom he has confidence and with whose methods he is familiar. The family doctor may also provide the psychiatrist with initial information about the family background. In the event that no family doctor is available, a friend may suggest a psychiatrist who has helped a relative or an acquaintance.

In the United Kingdom the position is a little different. Every person should have a general practitioner who may be consulted in emergency. The general practitioner will make an appropriate assessment and may decide to refer the patient to a psychiatrist working in a hospital setting. That hospital would normally be the hospital which serves the area in which the patient resides. Where this service proves inadequate the patient or his family may seek the advice of a psychiatrist practising privately, or, as in the United States, may contact the National Association for Mental Health who will advise them appropriately. A further area where help may be provided is the Casualty Department of the local general hospital. Most such departments have emergency psychiatric cover and in some of the major cities there are twenty-four-hour emergency psychiatric services provided at specific hospitals. With the exception of a private referral all these services are available under the National Health Service.

When the psychiatrist has been reached, it is important to stress whether the patient's condition seems to require urgent intervention or not. A layman's evaluation is not always accurate, but in a large number of cases it is a fair representation of the state of the patient. As a consequence of what he hears, the psychiatrist will determine whether or not the patient has to be examined right away. Nowadays general psychiatrists are very busy and often do not have time available for a few days or even a few weeks. They devote a great deal of their time to problems that do not constitute emergencies, to consultations or therapy with persons who seek a more fulfilling life or who have marital, vocational, or scholastic difficulties. If the psychiatrist realizes that the patient has to be treated as soon as possible and he has no time available or cannot make time available by postponing less pressing cases, he will provide the names of colleagues who he knows have openings.

It is useful to know how to distinguish a state of urgency from a state of emergency. A state of urgency implies a serious condition, but generally not one for which immediate action is of vital importance. A state of psychiatric emergency, on the other hand, requires immediate attention – within twenty-four hours or less. Conditions of emergency are relatively rare in psychiatry in comparison to other medical fields. Emergencies in reference to schizophrenia will be dealt with in Chapter 10.

Choice of Treatment

When the doctor sees the patient, he first has to determine whether the case requires immediate hospitalization or only office (out-patient) treatment. He has to make an assessment of the situation, based on his evaluation of the patient's condition at the time of the consultation and on the information that relatives or friends give him. At times more than one visit is necessary to reach a decision.

Two decades ago almost all patients who showed symptoms of schizophrenia were hospitalized, but this is not a common practice today. Today a patient is hospitalized when no better treatment is available or feasible outside a hospital, when a change to a hospital environment is necessary, or when the treatment available outside a hospital is not considered sufficient to control the symptoms to a level compatible with social life. We shall describe the criteria for hospitalization and hospital treatment in greater detail in Chapter 7.

In this chapter we shall discuss the two major types of treatment that can be given in the office of the therapist: psychotherapy and drug therapy.* These two types of treatment can also be given in a hospital setting, of course, and they generally *are* given to hospitalized patients. We shall omit any reference in this book to electric shock treatment and insulin treatment, which are now given very seldom and only in those few cases that do not respond to other therapies.

Although readers of this book do not intend to be therapists of schizophrenic patients, some understanding of the aims and procedures of these treatments will enable them to follow what the therapist is trying to do and will help them to build an atmosphere of confidence, warmth, and sober expectation with which to surround the patient.

---

* In the United Kingdom the availability of psychotherapy on the N.H.S. varies enormously from region to region. In some regions such treatment simply will not be available.

Psychotherapy and drug therapy are generally administered at the same time by most therapists today. There are some professionals, however, who administer mainly one or only one of them. The simultaneous administration of psychotherapy and drug therapy offers the possibility of attacking the psychological basis of the condition and of diminishing through biochemical means the intensity of the symptoms.

When a therapist has decided what course of action he will take – that is, what treatment or combination of treatments he will provide for the patient – the family must respect his decision and allow him to go ahead without interference. With the exception of psychosurgery, not to be recommended for anybody, the therapist must be allowed to embark on whatever therapeutic program he has selected. Later on, of course, the results must be evaluated.

Psychotherapy and drug therapy are generally given simultaneously, but we shall take them into consideration separately.

Psychotherapy

Although many types of psychotherapies are available (persuasion, hypnosis, behavior therapy, gestalt therapy), it is generally a psychodynamic therapy that is used in the treatment of schizophrenia.

Psychodynamic psychotherapy attuned to the schizophrenic is different from classic Freudian psychoanalysis in many respects. It may not require four or five sessions a week, but a schedule arranged according to the needs of the patient. Unlike psychoanalysis, it does not require the use of the couch except in a few cases. The patient generally sits in a chair facing the therapist, who, as a rule, does not wait for the patient to talk spontaneously with the so-called method of free association. The therapist intervenes frequently and conveys the feeling of active participation.

A classic psychoanalytic therapy that requires mobilizing anxiety in order to make the neurotic patient move and grow is not suitable for the schizophrenic. Such a method (except perhaps for the mildest cases or for patients close to recovery) is not only not beneficial but is counterindicated, since it may do more harm than good.

We must point out, however, that psychodynamic therapy of any type is also of Freudian derivation, because it was Freud who taught that the psychological problems of a patient do not start when the first symptoms appear but have a long history, often going back to the early childhood of the individual.

Psychodynamics means the study of psychological forces. Events that occurred earlier in life, the interpretation that the patient made of them, the particular grouping of these events, and their sequence in time become factors or psychological forces leading to certain outcomes. Paradoxically, Freud – who did so much for the understanding and treatment of the human psyche – was the one who discouraged psychoanalytic therapy of schizophrenia, although he specified that perhaps in the future methods would be devised to adapt psychoanalytic therapy to schizophrenics.

Freud was probably the greatest of those who worked in the field of the human psyche, and yet he, too, like every human being, allowed himself to be persuaded by preconceived notions or by theoretical positions that he himself had formulated. Freud believed that the schizophrenic patient, in his deep withdrawal from the enivironment and in particular from people, could not establish the relationship with the therapist that is necessary for effective psychotherapy. It was one of Freud's first pupils, Paul Federn, who demonstrated that this point of view was wrong, and in pioneer fashion Federn began treating schizophrenics. After him several other therapists attempted this treatment and introduced many innovative procedures. In America the therapists who advanced the field of psychotherapy of schizophrenia have been Harry Stack Sullivan, Frieda Fromm-Reichmann, John Rosen, Harold Searles, Otto Will, myself, and many others. In England, important contributors have been Melanie Klein and her pupils H. Rosenfeld and D. W. Winnicott. Marguerite Sechehaye and Gaetano Benedetti in Switzerland have also made useful innovations.

The first task of the psychotherapist who treats a schizophrenic patient is not to gather information about his present or past history, as most doctors do on their first meeting with a patient. Certainly, it is important for the therapist to know as many facts as possible. What the family, friends, colleagues, or previous doctors can tell him is generally very useful. However, in his first contact with the patient, his purpose is to 'reach' him; that is, to establish an interpersonal rapport as close to normal as possible. This is not an easy task. As we have already discussed in Chapter 3, the patient is suspicious and distrustful. He considers any question an intrusion into his private life, part of a plot, or an attempt to deprive him of something that belongs only to him. In a few cases, questions are considered by the patient as tricks perpetrated on him to prove that he is sick, that he has to be locked up in an insane asylum, declared incompetent, deprived of his legal rights, and robbed of his freedom and property. The therapist must try to persuade the patient that he is there to help him to understand many things, especially the troubles that he has had recently, or the experiences that he has had and that others for some reason do not interpret as he does.

It is very difficult even for trained therapists to carry out the first phase of the therapy of schizophrenia, which consists predominantly of an attempt to establish an atmosphere of basic trust in or confident expectation of each other, such as there should be between people who not only are not afraid of each other but are willing to cooperate amicably toward the achievement of a common goal.

Previous chapters have shown how the patient has had difficulty in communing with people since early life. He was almost always ill at ease in his relationships with other persons. He was alert, on guard, or in a state of more or less pronounced tension. Although such feelings also exist in neurotics and to some mild degree even in normal people, they are particularly marked in the person who later becomes schizophrenic. We have already illustrated how these feelings become transformed into suspiciousness, paranoid attitudes, and most of all experiences of hostility coming from people in general, or some particular people, and eventually from those conceived as persecutors.

The therapist must pave his way along a path that will lead the patient to regain confidence in at least one human being. He must at first become an exception for the patient – not a person to be mistrusted like the others, but a person who is willing to share whatever anxiety and fears the patient has, and finally a person who nourishes (psychologically speaking), who interprets things in a different way, and most of all who relieves anxiety and inspires a hopeful expectation for the future. It is not necessary for the family, or even for the concerned layman, to know how the therapist will achieve these goals in the first part of the treatment. What is required of the family is to be patient and hopeful and not to ask the therapist unanswerable questions. For instance, they should refrain from asking whether he has understood the cause of that particular case, or what was the particular event in childhood that eventually led to a disastrous course, or the errors that parents have committed – in other words, whether he has found the key needed to unlock the secret of that particular case of schizophrenia.

The therapist who treats cases of schizophrenia may, during the initial stage of treatment, resort to methods that are not adopted in the usual practice of psychotherapy. He may hold the patient's hand, pat his shoulder, walk with him in the park, look at a book with him, have a cup of coffee with him, and so on. If the family hears about these procedures, they should not become alarmed at these apparently unprofessional methods or think that the therapist and patient are losing time or have developed too much familiarity, friendship, or closeness. Actually they are resorting to anything that spontaneity or sudden inspiration suggests. They try to get to know each other, to accept each other, and soon to respect each other as whole persons, independent of the various views and feelings on which they may differ.

Only when such rapport has been established will the psychotherapist be able to approach the main part of the patient's symptomatology, and only then will the patient permit the therapist to suggest a correction or offer different interpretations about what is happening in his life. In other words, at this more advanced stage of treatment the therapist must tackle what seem (to everybody except the patient) to be fantasies or imagination. This really means attacking the core of schizophrenia. How to convince a patient that the voices he hears are not really voices but are heard only by him, in his mind? How to convince him that the things he sees are not really there but are only in his mind's eye? How to convince him that people are not laughing at him, or talking behind his back, or plotting against him? He is like a person in a dream. The dreamer believes that the dream is real until he wakes up, or until he is about to wake up and starts to surmise that what he is experiencing is only a dream. How to wake up the schizophrenic from the dream he lives in when he is awake?

First of all, let me clarify certain matters. I said something that in some respects is inaccurate; that the dream is not real life. It *is* real life. To dream is part of our life. Moreover, as Freud was the first to show on a scientific basis, the dream, although substantially incorrect, has a basis in the life of the dreamer, or a meaning that is revealed only in a distorted way, a way that could be called symbolic, fictitious, hidden in a secret code. We could repeat the same thing about schizophrenic symptoms. We have already remarked that Carl Jung was the first psychiatrist to state that a schizophrenic person acts in life as a dreamer acts in a dream.

For the family of the patient or for the patient himself, it is not necessary to know psychotherapeutic techniques, except in the most general way. One of the common methods (and the one I follow) consists of pointing out to the patient what he does to himself when he thinks and feels in his own private ways. If the patient recognizes the special mechanisms that he uses, he may learn to intercept them, although with great difficulty at first.

For instance, with a methodology that I have devised, the therapist helps the patient to prevent the occurrence of hallucinations. Unless the patient has reached a degree of advanced regression, he can be guided to recognize that he does not hear voices all the time, but only when he expects them. If he catches himself in what I have called the *listening attitude*, he will be helped by the therapist to recognize all the stages of the hallucinatory experience and to intercept them. Until a short time ago, even experienced psychiatrists believed that hallucinations were not preventable. But this is not something in which the family can intervene directly; therefore I shall omit specifics on this important subject. However, as we shall see in more detail in another chapter, the family soon learns to recognize when the patient is hallucinating or is about to hallucinate. The facial expression, the position of the body, and the general attitude will be good clues. The only thing the family members can do is to engage the patient in conversation or start doing something with him, so that it will be more difficult for him to put himself into the listening attitude. Hallucinations and other schizophrenic symptoms have a tendency to facilitate their own recurrence. In other words, the more frequent they are, the more frequently they will recur, perhaps with increased momentum. They become habits so ingrained that they will reappear automatically at the least inner signal of anxiety.

The purpose of the therapist at this stage is also to understand the meaning of symptoms when they do occur. I shall present a few illustrations to show how this understanding is approached. They are taken from my book *Interpretation of Schizophrenia*.

A patient is taking a stroll in the park on a beautiful Sunday afternoon when all of a sudden peculiar events seem to him to take place. People sitting on the benches start to talk with great animation and to look at him strangely. They make some gestures that have obvious reference to him. Children who were running all over or playing in the nearby playground now run in the opposite direction to avoid being near him. An American flag that was waving in the distance is now drooping. All this is an indication that people think that a horrible man, perhaps a pervert who attacks children and women, is in the park. The patient is supposed to be that man. The news is spreading. He rushes back home in a state of intense, agonizing turmoil.

When he sees the therapist for the session and reports the incident to him, the therapist must understand the patient's need to construct such a fantastic picture. What happened before the patient went into the park? In what mood was he? Was he not looking for certain evidence? Did he not almost hope to find it, so that he would be able to explain that indefinite mood of being thought of as a horrible creature? He had an impelling need to transform a vague and diffuse menace into a concrete threat, to restrict to a specific event a spreading feeling of being humiliated, disparaged, discriminated against.

A great part of this stage of psychotherapy will consist of making the patient realize that he is not a passive agent, at the mercy of symptoms that seem to come from nowhere, but somebody who still has a great deal to do with what he is experiencing.

A relatively common occurrence is finding a fragment of truth in what seems irrational thinking on the part of the patient. Violet, a thirty-five-year-old single patient, was suffering from a relatively mild form of schizophrenia that permitted her to maintain a not inadequate social life and to keep her job in spite of her many symptoms. She had occasional hallucinations, some delusions, and numerous ideas of reference.

On her birthday Violet received a bouquet of roses from the company for which she worked. When she opened the package and saw beautiful yellow roses, instead of experiencing a happy feeling, she started to concentrate on the color yellow. The color is supposed to mean jealousy, and she felt that by giving her yellow roses people in the office wanted to let her know that they knew she was jealous of the wife of the boss. The following day she heard one of the workers humming the song 'The Yellow Rose of Texas,' and she felt this was done purposefully to expose her. Eventually everything that was yellow in color acquired the same meaning for her and had to be avoided. Finally she even disposed of two of her dresses, because they were yellow.

In her office there was a water-cooler that was out of order and that had to be hit in order to let the water flow. When people, and especially the boss of her department, were hitting the cooler, Violet thought they meant to hit her. When I asked her why she thought so, she said, 'I never walk. I run, like water, and I deserve to be hit!' I explained to her that when she was in a state of anxiety, she resorted to a special type of thinking to demonstrate her unworthiness, and that she attributed to others the feelings she had about herself. This explanation helped, and for some time there was considerable improvement, but then similar symptoms returned.

One day Violet came to my office in an angry mood and told me that the previous day her friend Lucy had come to visit her and had brought along her dog, a little cocker spaniel. She added, 'You see! She thinks my home is a doghouse. She thinks I am a dog.'

The patient also had the conviction that when her co-workers used the word *machine*, they were referring to her. She said, 'I work like a machine. I am sure they refer to me.' In fact, they actually were treating her as a machine, not as a person, by taking advantage of her efficiency and willingness to do a large amount of work without protest, like a machine. There is no doubt that people working in the firm had realized that her excessive work and compliance were due to some kind of abnormality in her personality, but nevertheless they took advantage of her condition. The bouquet of roses and other similar gestures were thus acts of compensation for exploiting her, but at the same time an acknowledgement that there was something unusual about her, symbolized by her being jealous of the boss's wife.

A reconsideration of Violet's symptoms disclosed that in her ideas of reference there was always at least a grain of truth. This grain of insight, however, remained minuscule. Nonetheless, the therapist can use this partial insight for therapeutic purposes. He explains to the patient that he is capable of seeing some truth. However, the patient cannot apply this insight to his whole life but only to the specific matter to which it refers. As in the case of hallucinations, the patient must change from a passive to an active role. In other words, we must exploit even grains of reality that are recognized in the midst of disturbed thinking, when these little pieces of reality disclose a remarkable understanding and sensitivity.

The benefit the patient receives from this method is not just the result of some kind of intellectual agreement between two debating persons. When Violet was approached by the therapist in the way we have described, she felt much better and no longer alone with her strange symptoms. She felt that the therapist really shared her feelings and ideas; he did not just pretend to do so. After that Violet started to improve; she became more socially adequate and was able to sustain close and enduring romantic relationships with men. At the age of thirty-nine she got married, and at the age of forty she had a child. The child is now over twelve years old, and the whole family is well and happy.

As we have seen, many delusional ideas of patients are based on lack of self-esteem or on a very poor opinion or image that the person has of himself. A common example is the patient who has the idea that people laugh at him. He actually hears them laughing. He turns his head; he looks at them and has the impression that they smile and ridicule him. They may not smile at all, and he may misinterpret their facial expressions. If they do smile, they may do so for reasons that have nothing to do with him. The therapist will help the patient to recognize that he sees or hears people laughing at him when he *expects* to see or hear them. When the treatment is more advanced, the patient recognizes that he feels people *should* laugh at him because he is a laughable individual. He hears them laughing because he believes that they should laugh at him. What he thinks of himself becomes the cause of his symptoms. It is painful for the patient to acknowledge that that is what he is, what he thinks of himself. In a later stage of treatment he will be helped, of course, to change this disastrous vision.

At times low self-esteem leads instead to symptoms grandiose in content. A person who considers himself Jesus Christ or St Paul or Einstein or a great inventor is a person who has an unconscious vision of himself that is very low, frequently horrendous. He tries to deny this vision by believing that he is superhuman or one of the greatest human beings living or dead.

In a more advanced type of therapy, when there is a rather intense closeness between the patient and the therapist, an attempt must be made to interpret the past history of the patient, with stress on those situations in childhood and in the family environment that were causes of conflict. Relationships, especially with parents, will receive great consideration. In a certain type of patient, one who used to be more common in the past and may become more common again, at the beginning of treatment the parents are described by the patient as saviors, angels, benefactors. The patient who is frightened of the world and still feels so dependent on the parents has the need to see them (more frequently the mother) in that extremely positive way. Any negative quality that the parent may possess is displaced to the persecutors.

The majority of patients, however, do not see their parents in this light. After the initial stage of treatment during which the patient focuses on the persecutors and sees the parents in a neutral way, he discovers the importance of childhood and of his relationships with mother and father. He then develops another attitude toward them. The original image of the parents that he had built in childhood comes to consciousness and he attributes to the parents full responsibility for his illness and despair. He is bound to manifest great hostility for the parents and to refer to them in the most uncomplimentary ways. As we have seen in a previous chapter, even some therapists have believed that these characterizations of the parents' personalities correspond to reality.

It is easy for the therapist to believe in the accuracy of the patient's accounts, first because a minority of parents *do* fit this negative image; second because the patients who had shifted their target from the persecutors to the parents had made considerable improvement, were no longer delusional or were delusional to a lesser degree, and seemed to a large extent reliable. Delusions are easily detected because they are far removed from reality, but distortions, as they occur at this stage of therapy, are difficult to recognize because they are only exaggerations or deformations of some elements of reality.

This period of treatment may constitute a more difficult test for the family of the patient than for the patient himself. Now the roles are reversed. It is no longer the patient who feels accused by imaginary people; it is the parents who feel accused by the patient. The only recommendation I can offer is to try to sustain this period with fortitude. Sooner or later, with the help of the therapist, the patient will come to recognize that he has exaggerated or deformed the role that his parents have played in his psychological difficulties. The therapist will need to help the patient distinguish what was really negative in the parents from what has been added to his vision of them, first by the special sensitivity of the patient, then by the particular sequence of events, third by the immaturity of the patient's understanding when these events took place, and finally by the illness itself.

In his newly developed antiparental zeal, the patient often goes on a campaign to distort what the parent does and says now. Incidentally, this tendency is present not only in schizophrenics but also in some people who show schizophrenic tendencies without ever reaching a degree of disturbance that justifies the diagnosis of schizophrenia. By being stuck in an antiparental frame of reference the patients may not need to become delusional. To a much less unrealistic extent this tendency occurs in some neurotics, too. At times the antiparental campaign is enlarged to include parents-in-law and other people who have a role similar to the parental one.

The therapist will help the patient to correct distortions and exaggerations in many ways, as I have described in my book *Interpretation of Schizophrenia*, but these need not concern us here. Of course, what has to decrease and eventually disappear is the need to distort, to have targets, to use scapegoats, to consider the limitations or undesirable qualities of one's life or of life in general as the responsibility of a few persons, at first of the persecutors, later of the members of the family.

Transference and Countertransference

There are many other aspects of psychotherapy that are beyond the scope of this book but that may nevertheless be useful to mention. First among them is the analysis of the transference, that is, the feeling that the patient has for the therapist. This analysis helps to understand not only the important relationships that the patient had with his parents in childhood, but also the relationships that he is able to establish now. The countertransference, or the feeling that the therapist has for the patient, is also important and has to be studied to clarify the feeling that the patient may evoke in people with whom he establishes a state of closeness. In the original classical psychoanalytic therapy, as devised by Freud, the analyst was not supposed to reveal or experience any countertransference or any feeling for the patient, who was supposed to remain a neutral object. This stance may be fruitful in the treatment of patients with the typical forms of neuroses described by Freud, but certainly not with the schizophrenic patient.

As Gertrude Schwing, a nurse analysand of Paul Federn's, was the first to write (in her book on her treatment of schizophrenic patients), the therapist must have a maternal attitude and disposition. He must not only interpret and point out distortions and displaced feelings but also nourish, in a psychological sense. Just as it is impossible for us to conceive of a good mother who nourishes her child as if he were a neutral object, without having feeling for him, it is equally impossible to imagine an effective psychotherapist who remains neutral toward his schizophrenic patient. The therapist will not be able to surmount the numerous obstacles unless he is motivated by a strong feeling of enthusiasm and awareness of what his mission requires.

One of the pioneers in the psychotherapy of schizophrenia, John Rosen, expressed this point of view very well when he wrote that in the treatment of the schizophrenic the countertransference must be similar to the feelings that a good parent has for a highly disturbed child. Rosen wrote that the therapist must identify with the unhappy patient as the good parent identifies with the unhappy child and be so disturbed by the unhappiness of the patient that he himself cannot rest until the patient is at peace.

The feelings of transference and countertransference do change, of course, as therapy progresses. The therapist is seen less and less as a person who has to be kept on a pedestal. Although he retains his authoritative (not to be confused with authoritarian) position in psychological matters, he becomes more and more a peer. A certain degree of closeness and intimacy is reached, which should not be confused with something else or be considered too invasive, too permissive, or as having sexual connotations.

The successful therapy is one that leads the patient first to lose his symptoms, second to find self-acceptance. Self-acceptance for the schizophrenic is the best indication of growth. It is only when the patient authentically accepts himself that we can be comfortably sure that he will not have relapses. In the successful course of therapy we witness this evolving sense of genuine self-acceptance (which should not be confused with false self-acceptance based on blaming others). We have seen that at the beginning of the illness the patient did not want to accuse himself anymore, did not want to reject himself anymore, and gained a pseudo-self-acceptance by accusing others – also by becoming Jesus Christ, Einstein, Queen Elizabeth. This, of course, is a psychotic self-acceptance, which needs delusions and special abnormal ways of thinking to be sustained.

Genuine self-acceptance necessitates seeing oneself differently from the way one did before the illness, but without resorting to delusions. It means having a stable self-image with more self-esteem, more hope about life and the future, and a different vision of the world, which also includes acceptance of one's limitations and those of mankind. In an atmosphere of relatedness the patient and the therapist constitute a team that at first searches for, then discovers, then curbs the old and rigid patterns and lastly reconstructs and veers toward directions that were unknown before. All this requires innumerable applications of details whose specifics are beyond the scope of this book.

It is clear, however, that the basic philosophy or ultimate aim of the psychotherapist is different from that of any other physician or therapist. The usual aim of the physician is to bring about what in medical schools used to be called *restitutio quo ante*, a return to the premorbid condition, to the state the patient was in before he became ill. This principle is a valid one in general medicine. The doctor wants to bring back the patient to the condition he was in before he developed pneumonia or mumps or broke his leg. The psychotherapist of the schizophrenic wants more than a return to a premorbid state, because the premorbid state of people who have become schizophrenics was already morbid and had many non-schizophrenic and preschizophrenic characteristics that made the patient vulnerable. Of course, sometimes we have to settle for less, for many cases respond only partially to psychotherapy. In Chapter 9 we shall describe in detail the various outcomes of treated schizophrenia.

Before we terminate this discussion of psychotherapy, it is important to note that some therapists recommend group psychotherapy. In my experience, group psychotherapy is a valid and desirable adjunct in many cases of schizophrenia, but it does not replace individual psychotherapy.

Drug Therapy

There are many therapists today who believe that schizophrenia is a biochemical disorder of the brain. Other psychiatrists believe that the biochemical alteration is a consequence and not a cause of schizophrenia, just as a disorder in the metabolism of carbohydrates is the consequence of diabetes and not the cause.

There is little doubt, however, that whether they are causes or effects, biochemical alterations do occur in the brain of the schizophrenic. Many psychiatrists attempt to correct these biochemical changes, or rather, to neutralize some effects of these changes, by administering special drugs. Even a psychiatrist who gives much importance to psychological factors (as I do) uses drug therapy in the treatment of many patients. Drug therapy offers a number of advantages when it is used with psychotherapy. It produces a sense of distance between the patient and his symptoms. The patient is less involved with what disturbs him, relates more easily to the therapist, and is able to listen to him and to keep in mind the meaning of what he says. In acute conditions, characterized by extreme restlessness, agitation, and incoherence, the patient cannot attend to the therapist or even notice his presence. No rapport is established unless he is calmed down by drugs.

In some cases the decrease in the intensity of symptoms makes hospitalization unnecessary. The patient continues to work and is able to obtain psychotherapy on an ambulatory basis, that is, in the office of the therapist. When psychotherapy is utilized simultaneously, no massive doses of drugs should be given lest the patient become insensitive to the interpersonal approach.

In cases for which psychotherapy is not available or available only to a minimal degree, drug therapy is still useful and in a large percentage of cases brings about disappearance of the obvious symptoms, such as hallucinations, delusions, and ideas of reference. The patient is in better contact with the world and better able to take care of himself and provide for his personal needs. At times residues remain, and the symptoms may reappear in conditions of stress. Critics of drug therapy point out that this form of treatment removes only the symptoms, and that the patient is left with the same personality and the same character structure as before. Drugs do not make him change his image of himself, life, the world, the future. The genetic predisposition is also unchanged, they say; thus the patient remains vulnerable to future attacks and retains the same potential for illness. This is true only to some extent. A patient who has shed his symptoms may be helped by fortunate circumstances to face life again in more constructive ways. Moreover, we should not minimize the importance of eliminating symptoms when such symptoms are incapacitating – as catatonic features, hallucinations, delusions, or thinking disorders can be – or when the general behavior of the patient is bizarre. It is important for the patient and the family to know that in a satisfactory environment (see Chapter 8) drugs do prevent relapses even without psychotherapy. Prevention of relapses does not signify that the patient has reached a desirable state of maturity, however, or lasting immunity to the illness.

At the beginning of the sixteenth century Garcia de Orta, physician to the Portuguese viceroy, described in his *Coloquios* the effects of a drug with which he had become familiar during the thirty years he spent in the Far East. His observations on the effect of extracts from the root of *Rauwolfia serpentina* might have been forgotten had not the French physician Charles de l'Escluse, known also by the Latin name of Carolus Clusius, disseminated the findings in a book that was published in Latin in the year 1567. Rauwolfia was named after Leonard Rauwolf, a German physician and botanist who toured the world to study medicinal plants.

In 1952 Swiss biochemists isolated from the roots of Rauwolfia a substance they named *reserpine*. It was soon discovered that this substance produced a beneficial effect on schizophrenic patients. During the same year Charpentier in France synthesized chlorpromazine, a product that soon proved even more effective than reserpine.

Chlorpromazine is a phenothiazine. The phenothiazine nucleus had been synthesized in 1876 with the development of such aniline dyes as methylene blue. Before I became a full-time psychiatrist, I did neuropathological studies; that is, I did research, gross and microscopic, on human brains. At that time the main method for coloring nervous cells in histological sections of the brain was the Nissl method, which used methylene dyes, and especially thionine and toluidine. It never occurred to me that one day a substance chemically similar to those used to stain dead brain cells would serve to benefit mental patients. And yet the great Nobel prize-winner Paul Ehrlich, who developed the theory of specific drug-tissue interaction, had suggested as early as the 1890s that methylene blue might be used in treating mental illness.

It is not necessary for the reader to know the various compositions of the drugs used for schizophrenia. However, for those who are somewhat acquainted with biochemistry, I wish to state that a phenothiazine contains a tricyclic nucleus of two benzene rings, connected through a central ring which contains a sulfur atom (S) and a nitrogen atom (N). Attached to the nitrogen atom is a carbon side chain (R_1), which is either tertiary amine or a structural equivalent.

It is also not necessary for the reader to know the chemical structure of the various drugs used in the treatment of schizophrenia. But I shall mention here for those who are interested some of the most commonly used products and the names (in parentheses) under which they are marketed by pharmaceutical firms: thioridazine (Mellaril), fluphenazine (Prolixin), perphenazine (Trilafon), trifluoperazine (Stelazine), chlorprothixene (Taractan), thiothixene (Navane), loxapine (Loxitan), haloperidol (Haldol), and molindone (Moban).

There is a great variety of responses to these drugs. Thus the amount to be given daily or in each dose has to be determined by the doctor for each individual patient. When the dose is taken orally, effects appear within thirty to sixty minutes. One of the great advantages of these drugs is that they are not addictive and thus are in no way comparable to such substances as barbiturates, chloral hydrate, or amphetamines. For patients who are forgetful or careless in taking the accurate doses at proper times, an injection of a powerful dose of fluphenazine (Prolixin) can be given. When adminstered as maintenance therapy, a single injection may control symptoms for up to four weeks.

Unlike megavitamin or orthomolecular treatments of schizophrenia – which, according to my experience and that of many other psychiatrists, are totally ineffectual – antipsychotic agents such as those I have mentioned above produce a definite effect. They are able to eliminate or ameliorate the symptoms in the majority of cases. After the disappearance of the symptoms, drug therapy should not be discontinued but prolonged for at least several months, in decreasing dosages. It will be up to the physician to determine with periodical trials when to diminish the doses or discontinue them altogether. The best way is to continue treatment until the psychiatrist believes that the danger of relapses is markedly diminished.

The mechanisms of action of these antipsychotic drugs are not known. We have a few clues, but they have not been adequately put together and their interpretation is controversial. Unlike the barbiturates, which act mainly on the cerebral cortex and on the respiratory centers in the medulla, the phenothiazines and other antipsychotic drugs act mostly on subcortical structures of the brain, the reticular formation, midbrain, hypothalamus, rhinencephalon, and basal ganglia. By acting on these subcortical areas antipsychotic drugs diminish arousal of the central nervous system without reducing significantly the functions of the cerebral cortex and therefore trigger practically no impairment of the higher (cognitive) functions of the mind. These drugs also have the capacity to decrease the input of stimulation that becomes excessive or too much to master in acute psychotic conditions. They seem to diminish the functions of the sympathetic nervous system.

Another important characteristic of antipsychotic compounds is that they are relatively safe. It is practically impossible to commit suicide by ingesting a large quantity of them. However, we should not consider them harmless. Also, we must keep in mind that the effect of prolonged use is not completely known. The doctor in charge of the patient requests periodical blood counts, because in a small minority of patients the drugs adversely affect the blood formula. Also, the liver and other parts of the organism may be harmed.

Two types of side effects occur frequently and should always be kept in mind. One type consists of symptoms called *extra-pyramidal*. The patient may develop a stiff face, posture, and gait. Spontaneous movements of arms and legs are curtailed and in some cases the patient may also have rolling of the eyes and tremor. These side effects are generally corrected with medications such as benztropine (Cogentin), procyclidine (Kemadrin), and trihexyphenidyl (Artane).

Another group of unpleasant side effects, included under the term *tardive dyskinesia*, appears in a minority of patients after they have received antipsychotic agents for a long time. These effects consist of involuntary movements of the lips, tongue, face, and other parts of the body. They are more difficult to correct than extrapyramidal signs.

All these side effects remind us that drug therapy should not be given indiscriminately, but with caution and with the intention of terminating the treatment as soon as possible.

7. Hospital Therapy

Hospitalization: For and Against

In spite of several changes in its evaluation and application, hospital therapy retains a very important role in the treatment of schizophrenia. Modern psychiatric hospital therapy has a long history that we can only touch upon here.

Following French psychiatry, American psychiatric hospitals were organized at the beginning of the nineteenth century to provide so-called moral therapy. At that time psychological factors contributing to mental illness were called *moral causes,* and moral treatment consisted of humanitarian care in a hospital setting. The aim was to make the patient feel comfortable, to arouse his interest, and to promote friendship with others and discussions of his difficulties. Activities within the hospital structure were planned to be purposeful. The moral therapist acted toward his patient as if he were not ill, expected him to behave in a normal way, and treated him with dignity.*

Moral treatment is very similar to what is attempted today with hospital therapy. Unfortunately, after the Civil War moral treatment declined. Large state hospitals were organized with the intention of eliminating abuses to which the mentally ill were subjected in various parts of the country, but they soon became overcrowded and acquired unpleasant characteristics of their own. Until the early 1940s, state hospitals generally offered protection and custody rather than therapy. More was done to separate the patient from society than to rehabilitate him, since society at that time was unduly fearful of any form of bizarreness and deviance.

*For a detailed and accurate account of moral therapy, see J. S. Bockhoven, *Moral Treatment in American Psychiatry* (New York: Springer, 1963).

The negative characteristics of the hospitals were to a large degree due to the fact that psychiatry did not have much to offer in the form of therapy, but also to the fact that administrators were under constant pressure from state governments to spend as little as possible of the taxpayers' money.

The situation is drastically changed today. Psychiatric hospitals, whether private or public institutions, are much better equipped, although some still leave much to be desired. Many patients, as well as a considerable number of psychiatrists, are reluctant to use hospital facilities unless the choice is absolutely necessary. This attitude is partially an emotional sequel to what was known about some hospitals of the past, but it is also due to the fact that even the best hospital in the world places some limitations on the freedom of the individual.

Most psychiatrists think that such limitations should not be imposed unless absolutely necessary. Some, but very few, feel that hospitalization should *never* be imposed, even if it seems necessary for restoring the patient's mental health. The patient must give his full consent. The point is that a certain number of schizophrenics (fortunately not the majority) are so affected by their mental condition that they do not realize that they need to be hospitalized. Most psychiatrists, however, have learned from their clinical experiences that once the patient recovers or improves to a considerable extent, he is grateful for having been placed in a hospital environment, where he was treated and protected from his destructive impulses. Conversely, he will be resentful if – even for the sake of respecting his will – people did not take adequate measures to protect his life, his physical health, and the restoration of a stable mental condition. Of course, whenever possible, efforts should be made to convince the patient to seek admission to a hospital on a voluntary basis.

As I have already indicated, nowadays psychiatrists resort to hospitalization much less than in the past. Whereas until twenty-five years ago a person who disclosed minimal signs of schizophrenia was rushed to a psychiatric hospital, today the presence of schizophrenic symptoms is not itself considered an indication for hospitalization. Before hospitalization is recommended, alternative possibilities are considered. Is psychiatric treatment in the office of the therapist or in a clinic sufficient? Are some other resources available, either in the family or the community?

Hospitalization fulfills many requirements. We shall first describe the three major ones: protection and custody of the patient; observation and diagnosis; and therapy. We shall take the others into consideration later in this chapter.

Some patients may require protection from their own thinking and behavior and must be under some kind of benevolent surveillance. They may be harmful to themselves or others. If they cannot control themselves or if they act under the command of hallucinatory voices or delusions, they suspend their judgment about the advisability of actions that may bring about a great deal of harm. Thanks to drug therapy and timely psychotherapy, the number of these patients has greatly diminished.

A considerable number of patients require hospitalization because they are in a state of confusion and regression and are unable to take care of their basic needs. A patient who has refused food or fluids for more than thirty hours should be hospitalized, whether the diagnosis is schizophrenia, anorexia, or a combination of both.

Other criteria for hospitalization (not unanimously shared by psychiatrists) are refusal on the part of the patient to accept medication or the patient's fear that his bizarre behavior will injure his reputation, especially if he lives in a small town.

At times the diagnosis is uncertain. The patient may seem to suffer from schizophrenia, but he is instead under the influence of mescaline, hashish, marijuana, LSD, amphetamine, alcohol, or some other substance. At times there may be a suspicion that the patient suffers from an atypical or undiagnosed brain tumor, hydrocephalus, or some other neurological disease. Special tests and close observation, available only in a hospital, are necessary. Other reasons for hospitalization are:

1. To remove the patient from the usual environment where the

conflicts originated and are perpetuated, or where an atmosphere of misunderstanding and poor communication exists, with manifestations of hostility and rejection.

2. To provide relief to the members of the family who can no longer endure the state of tension and turmoil created by the patient. This situation is keenly experienced when children must be cared for or when a family member is sick or pregnant. At times the family is no longer able to provide for the patient because of limited financial resources.

3. To remove the patient who has had a remission from a previous psychotic episode and shows signs of decompensation or poor readjustment and seems in urgent need of a less demanding environment.

4. To provide the patient with a therapeutic community, to be described later. Group therapy and a special type of living and working environment may be needed more than individual therapy, or in addition to individual therapy.

5. To provide the patient who feels general malaise with the security of hospitalization. In most of the these cases the illness is already in action. The patient feels he is falling apart or is vaguely or even distinctly persecuted, and he seeks the refuge and protection of the hospital. In some cases, carefully selected by the psychiatrist, hospitalization prevents an exacerbation of the disorder.

6. To initiate treatment with massive doses of a potentially toxic drug. Administration of drug therapy in some cases is too complicated to be carried out at home. Thus careful observation is necessary for a certain period of time. In some rare cases that require electric shock treatment, hospitalization may be necessary for the patient's periods of forgetfulness and disorientation.

7. To aid the patient who is alone. Nobody is there to help him, and he is too withdrawn, skeptical, suspicious, or apathetic to ask for help.

Contraindications to hospitalization are the following:

1. The symptomatology is not severe. We must remember that

the presence of such symptoms as hallucinations, delusions, ideas of reference, or peculiar behavior is not in itself sufficient reason for hospitalization. These symptoms constitute grounds for hospitalization only when they bring about the conditions outlined above.

2. Psychotherapy and/or drug therapy are diminishing the symptomatology to such an extent as to negate the need for hospitalization.

3. The patient's condition can be expected to worsen if free social contacts are prevented.

4. Stopping work is experienced as a defeat and should not be resorted to unless necessary. While receiving treatment in an office or clinic the patient may continue to work and provide for his financial needs.

5. The patient is suitable for, and willing to receive, office or clinic treatment.

6. Environmental conditions, although adverse, can be changed with some efforts on the part of the family, patient, therapist, and social worker. It is possible to make them less demanding and less traumatic.

It may at times be difficult, even for the experienced psychiatrist, to evaluate all these criteria for or against hospitalization in a relatively short time and to reach a quick decision. In clear-cut cases, such as those of acutely ill or homicidal and violent patients, the indications are evident. Some cases are doubtful because indications may vary in a short period of time. Other factors at times hamper the psychiatrist in making a quick decision. For instance, in the presence of paranoid persecutory ideas, the danger that the patient constitutes to himself or others may seem very remote, and yet the therapist may be reluctant to assume even a little risk. Errors are unavoidable because each aspect of the problem can be weighed only approximately and according to criteria that are often subjective in nature. Society at large and the family in particular must accept the inevitability of some errors.

Hospitalization, although helpful in many cases, does not cure schizophrenia. It must be supported by specific therapeutic methods. Often, even when hospitalization is deemed necessary, the psychiatrist must overcome the objections of family members who rebel against the idea of a ' mental institution.' Such a reaction is a residue of a concept held long ago, as we have already discussed. The family must be told that decisions about what to do today should not be based on knowledge of what pertained to the past.

Different Types of Hospitals and of Hospitalization

Generally the psychiatrist in charge of the patient discusses with the family – or, preferably, with the patient himself – three possibilities: (1) psychiatric services of general hospitals; (2) private hospitals; and (3) state (or provincial) hospitals.

Unless family funds are adequate to provide prolonged treatment in a good private hospital, the general hospital is the best choice. As a matter of fact, the number of patients admitted to such facilities now exceeds the number of patients admitted for the first time to state hospitals. The patient will likely be less reluctant to go into a general hospital, whose name is generally not associated with mental illness. Further, psychiatric departments of general hospitals are generally set up to keep the patient only for a few weeks, usually no longer than three months. All efforts are concentrated on making the patient ready to return to his family, work, and community as soon as possible. Short-term hospital therapy has the main aim of helping the patient through a life crisis. The first goals are reduction of insecurity, anxiety, and confusion. Any psychotherapy is generally problem-oriented, does not delve into the past, and does not attempt to produce basic changes in the patient's personality.

The best general hospitals are those associated with medical schools, but this rule of thumb has many exceptions. Often the family complains that the doctors in charge of the patients are residents, too young to understand the complexity of a disturbed human psyche. There is some validity in these complaints. However, when the immediate need is to enable the patient to face the world again, without the necessity of a deep exploration of his psyche, the general hospital is usually equipped for the job.

Whatever remains to be done for the patient will be done later outside the hospital. Even when the patient is in a general hospital, however, other doctors – psychiatrists who supervise the residents – confirm or rule out the diagnosis of schizophrenia and discuss drug therapy. Psychotherapy is reduced to a minimum. The nurses and attendants generally do a very good job of creating the atmosphere of reassurance and protection that the patient needs to get through the crisis.

Treatment in a private psychiatric hospital is less expensive per diem, but it becomes much more expensive than a general hospital because of the length of stay. The aim here is not just to rehabilitate the patient to face the world, but also to start to understand his psychological difficulties and to attempt the re-integration of his psychological apparatus. Although there are some private psychiatric hospitals that have the same basic policy as general hospitals and aim at the shortest possible length of treatment, in the discussion here we shall consider those hospitals in which the brevity of the hospitalization is not a basic issue. A few hospitals are organized mainly as profit-making centers and therefore are undesirable. Most hospitals, however, range from adequate to good, and some are excellent. Those to be preferred are those particularly oriented to treating adult or adolescent schizophrenics and that do not accept children, old people, drug addicts, and alcoholics.

Whereas the basic aim of the general hospital is to eliminate the signs of acute decompensation (like refusal to eat or take care of oneself, incontinence, making faces, or screaming), the staff of a private hospital has learned to tolerate these signs of regression.

Long-term hospitalization is required when it is felt that the patient needs a stable environment in which he can shed his symptoms and achieve a sense of self-reliance. Either the intended short-term hospitalization did not bring about the desired effects, or improvement is slow or nonexistent, or previous short-term hospitalizations have ended in failure. The main goal of the hospital staff is to produce a basic change in the way the patient experiences himself, life, and the world. The staff is willing to give the patient the time necessary to achieve this goal. In some private hospitals, too, acute regression features are quickly combated, but the long-range goal is still the prevailing concern. Although drug therapy is used, some kind of psychotherapy is also instituted.

If the family has no funds for prolonged private hospital treatment, the patient may be admitted to a state hospital. Some have improved enormously, especially in treating schizophrenic patients. They are much less crowded than they used to be, since drug therapy has permitted discharge of many patients. Also, patients with organic conditions (senile, arteriosclerotic, and neurological cases) are no longer admitted in many of them.

Before 1955 the average stay in a state hospital was six months. The time spent in hospital has now dropped to around forty days (although, of course, a certain number of chronic patients remain there for years, some indefinitely). Although the population of hospitals has decreased, the number of admissions has increased to almost double what it was in 1955. Wards with incontinent, naked, aggressive, and screaming patients have all disappeared. Drug treatments have brought about these changes.

In spite of improvements, many state hospitals leave much to be desired. Because of limited funding, and also because relatively few physicians go into the field of psychiatry (and those who do prefer not to work in state institutions), state hospitals are almost always understaffed. Drug therapy is preferred to psychotherapy, and a great deal of the work falls into the hands of attendants. Even nurses are not found in sufficient number.

A complaint one often hears is that the majority of doctors working in state hospitals are foreigners who, because of linguistic difficulties, are unable to communicate fully with the patients. Psychiatric practice requires a more refined knowledge of the spoken language than other branches of medicine. There may be some validity in these allegations, but other factors also have to be considered. Certainly a deep knowledge of the prevailing language, with common colloquialisms and incidental references to expressions heard in nursery rhymes or during babyhood and kindergarten, is advantageous. On the other hand, it has often been observed that the foreigner, by the very fact that he is a foreigner, can better understand the schizophrenic, who feels like a foreigner in his society. The Latin word *alienus* and the derivative English word *alien* mean foreigner. It is not due to chance that *alienist*, also a derivative of the same Latin word, was once a term for psychiatrist. In the first therapeutic communities organized in England several years ago, it was felt that foreign personnel from Scandinavian countries related to the patients better than those born in England. Ability to compare the effect of two different cultures on the human psyche also offers the foreign-born psychiatrist unusual opportunities for a better understanding in some specific cases.

In the United Kingdom many of these comments also apply. The private hospitals occupy a less important part in the psychiatric services, as there are at present few private psychiatric hospitals. Many general hospitals now have psychiatric wards, but there are still large numbers of mental hospitals dealing only with the psychiatrically ill. Conditions in these hospitals vary considerably and many of the problems encountered in the United States will also be met in the British mental hospital. Furthermore, hospitals serve designated areas, and patients may have little or no choice of hospital to which they may be admitted. Some of the postgraduate and undergraduate teaching hospitals are not restricted to particular catchment areas and will admit patients from all over the United Kingdom. Patients who require long-term hospitalization are likely to be admitted, in the end, to mental hospitals. There are a number of experimental projects being mounted which involve the use of ward-hostel environments, day centers, day hospitals, and halfway houses where patients take progressive responsibility for themselves. These innovations are, however, relatively rare. Most patients will be obliged to find help within the mental hospitals of the National Health Service, where treatment is likely to be along conventional lines.

Milieu Therapy

The aim of the hospital is, of course, not just to offer shelter and protection and hasten the diagnostic procedure, but to provide treatment. In addition to the various types of treatment, each of which could be given outside a hospital setting but that in the hospital are all available at once if necessary, the hospital itself can be an instrument of treatment as a milieu or a special environment, which psychiatrist Maxwell Jones has called a *therapeutic community.*

Whereas in psychotherapy one patient understands himself better through his experience with another person, in the therapeutic community the total environment – the hospital setting as well as the people in it (patients, doctors, nurses, attendants, aides) – constitutes an atmosphere propitious to healthy relationships. The therapeutic community as a treatment has much in common with the moral treatment of the nineteenth century, to which we referred at the beginning of this chapter.

Maxwell Jones gives the following description of the therapeutic community:

There is much to be learned from observing the patient in a relatively ordinary and familiar social environment so that his usual ways of relating to other people, reaction to stress, etc., can be observed. If at the same time he can be made aware of the effect of his behavior on other people and helped to understand some of the motivation underlying his actions, the situation is potentially therapeutic. This we believe to be the distinctive quality of a therapeutic community. Clearly there is the possibility of any interpersonal relationship being therapeutic or antitherapeutic. It is the introduction of trained staff personnel into the group situation together with planned collaboration of patients and staff in most, if not all, aspects of the unit life which heightens the possibility of the social experience being therapeutic.

In the therapeutic community the individual patient is seen as an important member of the group. The emphasis is put on how he interacts with the group. Alan Kraft, in his article on the subject, explains how, through interaction, a network of communication develops in the community and 'includes communication of all kinds, manifest and latent, verbal and non-verbal, conscious and unconscious, and at all levels, patient–patient, patient–staff, and staff–staff. The perceptual and emotional distortions of communication in all relationships are scrutinized.'

The schizophrenic patient who has difficulties in communicating and relating may benefit greatly in such an environment. All the facets of the life of the patient are investigated and discussed openly and present opportunities for a living-learning experience. Kraft gives us a very good description of this type of milieu therapy when he writes that ' a therapeutic community is not unlike a school for living. The " student body" is composed of those who have found themselves unable to meet the demands of everyday responsibility. The " faculty" is the staff, who have developed skills and sensitivities which enable them to teach social skills and self-understanding. The " course work" consists of the daily living situation, similar in many ways to ordinary life situations but more protective and enriched to increase learning possibilities.'

In the therapeutic community there is a greater sharing of responsibility with patients than in usual hospitals. Patients participate in making decisions and a regular ' patient government ' is established. The patient's role is expanded with his improvement, and the fantasy of passively receiving solutions to his problems in a hospital setting is slowly altered.

Recently another form of milieu therapy, called *attitude therapy,* has been devised by J. C. Folsom. The treatment is based on five fundamental attitudes: (1) active friendliness, with which the patient is helped to move out of his isolation; (2) passive friendliness, when the therapist is available for friendship but makes no friendly overtures and waits for the patient to make the first move; (3) kind firmness, by which the therapist directs the patient into rewarding activities in a kind but firm manner; (4) matter-of-factness, or dealing with one another in a usual day-to-day relationship; and (5) no-demand attitude, used especially when the patient is in a state of panic of disintegration, and in which nothing is requested of him.

Hospital Services

Although most hospitals today try to retain at least some of the characteristics of the therapeutic community, many of them focus on the services they can render. Dexter Bullard, Jr, has prepared a list of services that a psychiatric hospital should provide:

Psychiatric diagnostic evaluation	Psychiatric nursing care
Individual psychotherapy	Behavioral modification therapy
Group psychotherapy	Activity therapy
Family therapy	Dance therapy
Social casework	Art therapy
Milieu therapy	Music therapy
Recreational therapy	Drug treatment
Occupational therapy	Physical therapies
Psychological testing	Medical and dental services
Educational testing	In-patient hospital services
Vocational testing	Day hospital services
Rehabilitation training	Night hospital services
Counseling	Out-patient services
Special educational services	Crisis intervention

Not a short list, although its author calls it 'partial.' Not all these services are required by every patient. The staff decides what is appropriate for a given individual. Unfortunately, in large hospitals procedures become standardized and a uniform approach sooner or later tends to be adopted.

In Chapter 6 we took into consideration psychotherapy and drug therapy. It is not necessary to learn the modalities of the various services listed by Bullard. We shall devote a few words, however, to three of them: behavioral modification therapy (or token therapy, art therapy, and dance therapy).

The method of 'token economy' was devised by T. Ayllon and N. H. Azrin and uses the technique of operant conditioning. By receiving tokens for such good behavior as work, grooming, bathing, brushing one's teeth, and so on, even the most regressed patients develop better habits and their management presents fewer problems. In my opinion, all the methods based on operant conditioning should be reserved only for the very sick who do not respond to other types of treatment. Unless interpersonal warmth is experienced, the system of reward and punishment may bring about improvement only on a behavioral level, without any appreciable change of the inner psyche.

Many schizophrenic patients start to paint spontaneously, even though many of them did not do so prior to their illness. It is impossible to verify the observation reported by some authors that schizophrenics paint more frequently than normal persons. Whether this is true or not, however, it is certain that the desire to paint noted in many schizophrenics contrasts with their frequent lack of involvement with the things of the world. Many hypotheses have been proposed to explain the phenomenon, but they are beyond the scope of this book.*

The artwork of schizophrenics may help us to hasten the diagnosis and to understand the nature of the illness. Since the pioneer work of Margaret Naumburg, † many professionals have learned to interpret paintings of schizophrenic patients as graphic representations of their conflicts. Some patients have difficulty in expressing themselves with words or in reaching certain levels of their psyche by introspective thoughts that require words. They represent their problems to themselves and others much better through their paintings and drawings. The art therapist helps the patient abandon stereotyped forms and assume an increasing freedom of expression. Art therapy has become very popular in many hospitals for at least two cogent reasons. It increases the patient's awareness of his conflicts and his ability to talk about them, and it promotes the patient's creativity and gives him a feeling of accomplishment and fulfillment.

Dance therapy is based on the assumption that the mind and the body must function in harmony. Any emotional illness brings about disruption and alteration of the movements of the body, especially those that express feelings. The greatest alteration of body movements occurs in the catatonic type of schizophrenia, but to a less pronounced degree it occurs in all forms of this illness.

* See S. Arieti, *Interpretation of Schizophrenia,* 2nd ed. (New York: Basic Books, 1974), pp. 351–74.

† Margaret Naumburg, *Schizophrenic Art: Its Meaning in Psychotherapy* (New York: Grune & Stratton, 1950).

Alterations of movement manifest dysfunction at preverbal levels.

Dance therapy increases awareness of one's own physique, promotes a better orientation towards one's body, and develops the pleasure of sharing movements with other persons. Dance therapists deal with such phenomena as gravitational pull, breathing, flow of energy, spatial patterns, special sequences of movements, and repetition of movements. By following group rhythmic movements patients become less concerned with their preoccupations, respond to external stimuli, and learn to act in harmony with others.

We could repeat for dance what was mentioned about painting. Some patients, by participating in group rhythmic activity, can externalize what they would never be able to express with words.

8. Living with the Patient Day by Day

Is Home the Right Place?

The patient who has been diagnosed a schizophrenic now lives with his family. He may be back from the hospital (or may have never been in a hospital). At least the acute episode is over (or there has never been an acute episode). At present the patient is well, almost well, or considerably better.

What does it mean to have a person who has been diagnosed a schizophrenic in the family?

With the recent and welcome trend to discharge the patient from the hospital as soon as possible, the role that the family can play at this point is again reasserted and reexamined with a different outlook. The emphasis is no longer on the family as a source of pathology, but as a major instrument of restoration to health. Even when the patient appears completely recovered, he must be considered vulnerable for a certain period of time and be treated with special considerations.

The family's participation in convalescence must be viewed in the greater context of rehabilitation. Rehabilitation is a subject we shall deal with in Chapter 9, where we shall take into consideration agencies that have been organized for this type of work: halfway houses, day hospitals and day centers, former-patients clubs, and even foster families. The family of the patient himself remains the most common, and in many cases the most valid, medium for rehabilitation. Many of the studies made by people who investigated the family as a source of conflict and abnormality can now give us insights on how the family can instead offer essential help.

The family can rehabilitate the patient but can not perform psychotherapy on him. There is a big difference in these two types of help, yet rehabilitation is often confused with psychotherapy or considered a form of psychotherapy. We have seen that psychotherapy helps the patient become aware of the reasons for his feelings and actions. It helps the patient to understand how symptoms are expressions of needs that he cannot accept and that have become unconscious. Psychotherapy also helps the patient to shed maladaptive patterns of behavior and to correct faulty ways of thinking. It would be too much to expect the family to attempt these arduous tasks. Whereas the psychotherapist and the patient engage in a common exploration of the inner life of the patient, the family members are engaged with him in an external exploration, in rediscovering that the external world is not so terrible as it once seemed but is a place where the patient, too, can find his own niche, and much more than that.

No theory has been formulated on how rehabilitation in the family, or with agencies outside the family, works. In reference to rehabilitation carried on outside of the family, we generally feel that it is effective when it makes available methods that facilitate the patient's relating normally to others, restoring faith in himself, and engaging in fruitful activities.

Relating normally to others includes having neighborly attitudes, interchanges with co-workers, and friendships, and beginning a search for intimacy and love. Restored faith in oneself means feeling an attitude of hope and promise towards one's present and future. Fruitful activities include common living, work, usual habits, and even play.

Although rehabilitation includes all this, perhaps the rehabilitation that occurs within one's family includes more, so that perhaps even the word *rehabilitation* is not appropriate in reference to the family. If we persist in using it, we would have to add that it is a special type of rehabilitation that includes reintegration in the family, not just restoring but also improving one's role in that close milieu. It involves familiarization or refamiliarization with one's own family, fraternization with siblings and other relatives – a warmer affective connotation than is thought of in connection with rehabilitation carried out by agencies.

But first, let us face squarely the reality of the patient's return home. A new factor has been added, and the family atmosphere is no longer the same. To make believe that everything is just as it was is masking reality; it requires the imposition of mechanisms of denial, which are soon likely to produce harm. Moreover, as we shall illustrate shortly, it is inadvisable for the family not to effect some changes. To recover from schizophrenia is not the same as recovering from mumps or measles. The development of a different climate is generally not a bad occurrence, but one that may be propitious to a satisfactory outcome. Living with the patient day by day becomes a therapeutic task, and, indeed, not an easy one even for the most cooperative family.

The first problem is to decide whether it is in the patient's best interest to live with the family. Although the decision is made with the participation of everyone involved, the main responsibility for it resides with the psychiatrist in charge. On this point various views are expressed in psychiatric circles. In a few of them the therapeutic role of the family is not appreciated at all, because it was within the context of the family that the patient's conflicts leading to the illness originated. The patient's family, the patient, and the patient's illness are seen in these psychiatric circles as a unit whose abnormality led to the undesirable result. There is no doubt that in a considerable number of cases this situation really exists. The intrafamilial conflicts are there, and the solution or even amelioration of them is so improbable that the best decision is for the patient to live separately from his family. Even when the psychiatrist thinks that the strong negative feelings the patient has for his family are unjustified and based only on his distortions, it is not advisable for him to live with the family until he sees his home milieu in a different way. Again it is important to stress that although the feelings may be founded on unrealistic premises, they are very real to the patient and must be respected. To do otherwise would be likely to lead to unfortunate results.

At other times the patient is genuinely willing to live with the family, but the psychiatrist decides against it because he feels that the particular family is not able to help the patient. Not everybody can. Some relatives, although they have good intentions, are too involved in their own problems, difficulties, illnesses, or demanding occupations to be able to participate in what is always a strenuous task. When the help of family members is not possible, the services of a therapeutic assistant or a psychiatric companion may be resorted to, as we shall discuss in Chapter 10. Caution is necessary in making these decisions because, although rehabilitation in the family may be the best, it may also be the most dangerous or risky. The family must offer not just a roof to shelter the patient but a hearth, a place where suffering and joy are shared in closeness and intimacy.

Introducing the Family to the Task

A larger number of patients and former patients continue to live with their families, either because the psychiatrist feels that the family environment is satisfactory or because it is the only one available. Not all psychiatrists prepare the family for the task, but I, among many others, believe it is important to give a general orientation. The aim is not to transform the family members into psychiatric nurses, but to make them understand better the problems that are involved so that they can add understanding to their affection and personal concern. I am always aware – and wish to make the family aware – that a family member has a great advantage over even the best nurse. For the family the patient will always be a person, not a clinical case. The relative already knows what the patient likes and does not like.

In my words of general orientation to the family members, I start by pointing out that human beings have learned since early childhood to deal with others, at least in the majority of our relationships, in ways that society or our particular milieu recommends. Society criticizes, rejects, or even punishes those who do not follow acceptable attitudes toward others. Acceptable attitudes generally reflect traditions many centuries old and have deep emotional roots in the lives of most individuals. They are maintained not only by example, imitation, and teaching, but also by methods of punishment and reward, or even by displays of power. Sociological attitudes have definite educational values, but they may have disastrous effects when they are imposed on or adopted by the schizophrenic patient or one who is recovering from schizophrenia. At least in the beginning of the convalescence, the family must exert these pressures as little as possible. The patient must feel accepted even if different and unconventional. To accept the patient as he is does not mean, however, to accept his behavior indiscriminately, as we shall see later. The patient must be integrated gradually into a structured life.

Most relatives insist that they never punish a patient who, having returned home, displays unconventional behavior. With great sincerity they state that they recognize that the patient's behavior – even when offenisve – is only the result of illness and that therefore they do not consider him accountable. The truth is that, unless they train themselves to do otherwise, they do punish the patient in subtle ways – that is, in ways that may be unnoticed by them but are obvious to the patient, who is particularly sensitized to any unpleasant input from the environment. The family member may punish the patient by avoiding him or by staying with him as little as possible; by not talking to him or by talking in brief, curt sentences; by refusing to listen to him or to give him explanations; by having a condescending, patronizing or superior attitude; by being in a hurry in every interchange with the patient; by showing a perplexed, annoyed, bored, or disapproving facial expression; or at times even an air of consternation. The family member should observe not only the behavior and attitude of the patient, but also his own – especially his own.

Let us assume that the brother of the patient really wants to be kind, helpful, and reassuring. Instead of being grateful, the patient who just returned from the hospital becomes distrustful, possibly contemptuous and hostile. It is normal for the brother to react by becoming annoyed, perhaps angry and condemnatory. In his turn the patient senses that his brother has such feelings, and thus he finds reinforcement for his attitude of distrust and hostility. The vicious circle may repeat itself. Of course, the brother must train himself not to respond in the way considered normal, but to realize that the patient still has a great need to project his inner turmoil onto others, and to blame them for it.

This example explains the complaint we often hear from the members of the family: 'I want to be genuine, authentic. Since Jean came back, I have to watch every word I say to her. I can't be spontaneous any more. But I don't know if what I'm doing is right. Maybe by being artificial like this I'm doing some harm. I believe in being authentic.' Such doubts, posed to oneself or to the psychiatrist, are legitimate and worthy of full consideration. The relative must analyze further what he means by authenticity. To watch one's words before talking to Jean does not necessarily mean to lose one's authenticity. But to act as if a serious illness had not occurred to a person dear or close to us is not to live authentically. It is authentic and more beneficial to realize that on account of the patient's particular vulnerability and sensitivity, we must modify some of our ways and refrain from using words or phrases that may sound ambiguous or even threatening to him. Moreover, let us remember that in recognizing the areas of vulnerability and great sensitivity of the patient, we may discover where and how we have been unintentionally insensitive, and perhaps even callous. We may recognize that we have wanted to impose our ways because we have considered them more appropriate, more efficient, more in agreement with what society expects – or simply because we like them better.

Living with a schizophrenic or with a person recovering from schizophrenia requires our utmost effort to consider that person and all his rights, and to accept his need to nourish special wishes. This is difficult to do even with a normal person who lives with us. With the schizophrenic it is much more difficult because of our almost automatic desire to help by giving advice, by teaching, by correcting the manifestations of the illness, and by preaching conformity.

We must recognize also that it is harder to help a sick adult than a sick child. With a child we feel relatively at ease in giving instructions or direct advice and in assuming an active role. We are reluctant to do so with an adult, lest he interpret our concerned attitude as unwarranted solicitude or as acknowledgement of his helplessness, childishness, and irrationality. Excessive parental care may actually be experienced as an insult and may reinforce the low opinion the patient has of himself.

Another bad habit, which fortunately is found in very few

families, is that of regarding what the patient says as utterly nonsensical and at times even funny.

From what we have learned in this book, it is evident that remarks and complaints made by the patient must be listened to and evaluated with respect. Fears and delusions are real, vivid, and almost always unpleasant experiences for the patients, even if they are based on complicated mechanisms that only the psychiatrist understands. If the family member does not understand what the patient says, he must at least respond to his request for attention and to his desire to start a dialogue. To the extent that he is capable, the relative must influence and guide the patient, not by suppressing his activities but by increasing his knowledge and clarifying difficult situations. As we have already mentioned, the cooperative family member gradually increases his awareness of the patient's sensitivity; he becomes more alert to what may affect the patient unfavorably. His 'antennae' must be ready to capture what is disturbing; he must be on the alert, but not too solicitous or too eager; he must remain near enough to give when the need is there, but distant enough not to scare the patient when he is not yet capable of accepting warmth.

Following Harry Stack Sullivan's terminology, we can say that the patient who cannot yet accept too much warmth may put into effect a malevolent transformation and interpret the offer of warmth as concealing ulterior motives. A family capable of tolerating the difficulties inherent in living with a convalescent schizophrenic is a very important factor in a favorable outcome. Although there may be one person who is more involved with the patient than the other family members, the whole family must interact and offer mutual support. In an atmosphere of solidarity it will be easier to offer an accepting and stable environment. In this therapeutic milieu the patient is welcomed and respected, almost like a prodigal son. He is accepted, no matter how he is or how he was. Concern, patience, endurance, and a selected form of permissiveness prevail. A sense of hopefulness about the patient's ability to change, and confidence in his ability to grow, is felt in the air.

An attitude of acceptance, although allowing a considerable

degree of permissiveness, should not extend to an unlimited laissez faire attitude. In a warm atmosphere that does not resort to rejection, punishment, belittling, or ridicule, the patient generally understands what kinds of actions are appropriate for him. Threatening to send him back to the hospital if he does not behave is extremely disturbing to his morale. If the problems are too difficult, if in spite of everybody's goodwill interpersonal tension increases, if there is a possibility of suicide or of violence, rehospitalization must be seriously considered. It should not be presented to the patient as a form of punishment, but as a need for an environment much more programmed and structured than a home can be.

It is fair to say that often the task is too big for the family, unless, in addition to the individual therapy of the patient, family therapy is resorted to.

Family Therapy

Many authors have reported that family therapy makes relapses much less frequent, shortens the length of therapy for the individual patient, and ameliorates the general conditions of the family, even independently of the illness of the patient. So far I have not stressed the role of family therapy. This is partially due to the fact that, unfortunately, only a small minority of families are willing to undergo this type of therapy. At times some members are willing, but not the whole family. In a large number of cases the financial conditions permit therapy only for the convalescent patient.*

As we mentioned in Chapter 4, family difficulties are not the only cause of schizophrenia, but at this stage of our knowledge they are considered one of the main factors. The resolution of these difficulties may not be as effective as it might have been during the childhood of the patient or prior to the onset of the illness, but it can still be dynamic enough to change favorably the environment in which the patient still has to live for a considerable amount of time. Family therapy may answer the following questions: Are the family's denials, distortions, and myths still operating against the

---

* Fortunately such considerations do not apply in the United Kingdom where there is a National Health Service.

patient's recovery? Is the family still divided by a schism, as psychiatrist Theodore Lidz described? What kind of communication occurs between the members? Is there a pseudo-dialogue or a real dialogue? Mutuality or pseudo-mutuality? Genuineness or games?

Although family therapy is strongly advocated when possible, the family must try in any case to become a therapeutic milieu, and I believe this is possible in many cases.

Some therapists have recommended that not only the immediate family but also intermediate or distant relatives like aunts, uncles, cousins, and grandparents be involved in the reintegration of the patient. Whenever possible this attempt should be encouraged. (Unfortunately, very seldom have I been able to implement this procedure. Perhaps my lack of success is due to the fact that my practice originates almost exclusively from a large metropolitan area where the clan type of family has practically disappeared.)

Families reduced to a few members or to a 'nuclear' group often do not have close ties with distant or intermediate relatives; relatives may not feel very much like going out of their way to help a patient whom they do not know very well. For accuracy's sake I must add, however, that I have occasionally found loving grandparents who have done excellent work with teenage grandchildren.

Specific Issues

Before describing modalities for living with a convalescent schizophrenic, we must stress again that each case is different; each constitutes a unique circumstance in an environment that is not exactly identical to any one observed before.

We shall now take into consideration specific issues that come up rather frequently in living day by day with the patient. In previous chapters we have already referred to an important and rather frequent development. The patient who used to be delusional is no longer so but still distorts many interpersonal relationships, sees them in a worse light than they are, and may be rather accusatory, especially toward his parents, whom he now considers the source of his misfortune. Other family members are also blamed, to a lesser degree. This is indeed hard to accept. The best attitude is not to argue with the patient or tell him that he is wrong. But it is difficult for many mothers and fathers not to be defensive. Their pride is hurt; they may become incensed and want to speak up in their own defense as vigorously as possible, as if they were on trial. If they yield to this tendency, the trial will go on and on, and progress will not be made. A good stance on the part of the parent is to say to the patient, 'Perhaps the time will come when you will see in a different way what we did and what we tried to do.' At the same time the parents can reassure the patient by stating that each member will see to it that the needs and rights of everybody are satisfied in the best possible way. The future then will have a great chance of being much better than the past.

Although the patient's impairments and areas of sensitivity should be taken into consideration, they should not be magnified. We should avoid making the patient more dependent than he is or treating him as an invalid or a baby. It is true that the activities of some convalescing patients are curtailed very much, but those of many are limited only minimally. We must fully exploit whatever is hardly touched or not affected by the illness. One of the main goals is to find a role for the patient within the institution of the family. Some chores must be assigned to him. This is generally easier for a female patient, but a male patient, too, must assume home responsibilities. The feeling that he is a contributing member of the family will be beneficial, and the residues of pity and discouragement that persists in the attitude of the family members will have a better chance to dissipate.

It has been noted that patients from poor families rehabilitate faster after their return to the family than patients from well-to-do homes. Wealthy persons tend to rely more on others for routine functions. In well-to-do families it is difficult to assign domestic chores to the patient. The patient must be encouraged to take care of his room, but it is also advisable not to restrict his activities to what is only his. On the contrary, it is advisable for him to engage in some activity that will benefit the whole family.

Often, especially immediately following his return from the hospital, the patient is not able to take the initiative. The relatives must be the initiators and must exercise a great deal of patience. It is a characteristic of partially recovered patients to do things at a much slower pace than the average person. Lack of concentration, inhibitions of all sorts, and intruding thoughts may interfere with any kind of activity. Nevertheless, if he continues to work on a steady basis and is encouraged for what he does, no matter how slowly, the patient will get a rewarding sense of satisfaction. As he gains confidence in himself the tempo of his actions will speed up.

One of the questions often asked is whether the patient, no longer satisfied with whatever roles and assignments were given in the home, should be given a job by relatives. Father and Uncle George own a big firm. Should Joe be employed there? At times a position happens to be vacant; at other times it can be easily created. Again we cannot give an answer applicable to all cases. A sound general principle is for a person with serious problems not to work for relatives. If the patient has reached a level of normality or near normality, he should be encouraged to work for other people. On the other hand, if he is very slow or cannot adjust to a schedule that requires getting up early in the morning and completing diversified activities, it is advisable for the patient – at least on a temporary basis and purely for pragmatic reasons – to work for a parent or relative who is more willing to accept his slowness and possible irregularities.

It has been observed by many therapists that from the point of view of becoming capable again of engaging in useful activities, patients who return from the hospital to live with their wives or husbands fare much better than those who return to live with their parents. Generally spouses do not treat the patient as a very dependent person, are less willing to accept a state of passivity, and encourage the patient to resume an active role. Parents, on the other hand, are more inclined to resume the parental role and to foster excessive dependency.

The therapist is often asked, 'Should we push the patient to be active, or shouldn't we?' Again there is no single answer. With patients who are inclined to be passive, a little push is appropriate, but it must be in the form of a kind push, given with velvet gloves, and by no means an authoritarian command. The patient must be encouraged and praised for what he has accomplished, no matter how little or how slow the results seem. The opposite attitude is valid when the patient is willing to take steps for which he is not prepared: to go immediately back to his usual job, to look for a new position, to return to college to finish the semester, to live by himself in his own apartment, and so forth. Here a kind of delaying technique should be applied. The patient is advised only to postpone these plans until he is able to meet the challenge more efficiently. He should by no means be discouraged but only invited to remake his plans in phases that succeed one another more slowly. In the meantime he must be stimulated to exploit whatever assets he has that may be used in the home, from simple errands for the family to the family's more complicated accounting.

In dealing with some families, we have other types of problems. Their expectations are really too high as far as the patient is concerned. We have already mentioned that the spouse is generally more prone than the parents to stimulate the patient to an active role. Although this generally has a favorable outcome, it may also be detrimental if the spouse's expectations are excessive for the patient who is recovering from an acute episode. A wife may expect the husband to become the provider again right away; the husband may expect the wife to fully resume her maternal duties. Accepting the fact that a return to health requires a longer period of time will relieve tension, impatience, and discouragement.

A common complaint, especially among young couples, is that the convalescing patient has become sexually inadequate. If the spouse of the patient is reassured as far as the future is concerned, he or she will be able to tolerate better the temporary inconvenience. Generally lack of sexual interest is due to a variety of causes. The most frequent is the medication that the patient may still take. Several neuroleptics diminish sexual desire, especially in the male, and may even prevent ejaculation. Some psychiatrists inform the patient that diminished desire is likely to occur and reassure him or her that it is a transitory phenomenon that will disappear with a decrease in the medication, any interruption of medication, or a shift to another drug. Many psychiatrists, however, neglect to inform the spouse, who has to be reassured, too, that the phenomenon is not permanent.

Lack of sexual interest, of course, may be due to the fact that the patient has not been concerned at all with sexual matters and has for a long time focused attention elsewhere, so that he or she has not developed a craving or has even become used to sexual abstinence. In other cases that patient may have to reappraise his or her relationship with the spouse and must know where he or she stands. It is advisable, of course, for the spouse to suggest to the patient that insecurity, anxiety, or unresolved hostility be discussed with the therapist.

One thing is certain and must be expressed in clear terms. It is not true that the recovering schizophrenic is in a state of anhedonia, as a few psychiatrists once thought. *Anhedonia* means inability to experience pleasure, including sexual pleasure. The patient is indeed able to experience pleasure fully, once he or she recovers or improves to a considerable extent and, as a matter of fact, may experience sexual pleasure to an intense degree never sustained before the onset of the illness. A certain group of patients has an increase in sexual appetite from the onset of the illness and retains it throughout the illness.

Involvement and Overinvolvement

Consultations with the therapist will help the family and the patient avoid the opposite dangers of overstimulation and understimulation, of being in an environment that offers and expects too much or too little. It is indeed difficult at times to find the proper balance. Overstimulation obligates the patient to cope with an environment beyond his ability. If the patient is withdrawn, lackadaisical, or seemingly oblivious, his well-intentioned relatives try to interest him in a thousand different ways, for instance, by taking him to movies, museums, and theaters; and by talking and talking and recounting stories of the good times spent together in the past. The patient may feel overwhelmed, especially if he has just returned from a hospital where, in spite of the therapy and the occupational activities, he felt alone. It may be very strenuous for him to try to adjust to a situation that requires overinvolvement or exposure to frequent conversation.

If the patient at this point says, in reference to his home, 'This is not my place,' or 'I feel pushed around,' these words are danger signals. The relatives must realize that this is the time to get off the patient's back, so to speak, or at least to loosen the ties with him.

Some British authors have made a distinction between the *subjective burden*, that is, the family's estimate of the hardship imposed by the patient's presence in the home, and the *objective burden*, which was what the researchers considered their own objective estimate. According to these researchers, there was a discrepancy between the objective and the subjective estimate, in that the objective estimate was always greater than the subjective. In other words, according to these authors the burden was always heavier than the relatives were willing to admit. Of course, one can argue as to how really objective the estimate of the researchers was. An outsider's assessment of the family situation may also be subjective, due to the very distance from that situation, that is, the lack of intense feeling or involvement with the patient. At any rate, the fact that the objective burden was considered by these researchers as far greater than the subjective speaks well for the family of the patient. It indicates that, contrary to common belief, most families do their best to participate in the great work of rehabilitation of a dear one and are willing to endure the required hardship.

Related to the problem of overstimulation versus understimulation is the problem of overinvolvement. British authors, inspired especially by John Wing, who has studied this issue in depth, have reported that overinvolvement on the part of the family, including the expression of too much emotion, is conducive to relapse. He and his colleagues have written, 'Fifteen hours or more a week of face-to-face contact between a schizophrenic patient and a highly involved relative carried a strong risk of further breakdown.'

If closeness renews conflicts and prevents privacy, then of course we have the picture of overinvolvement described by Wing and his colleagues. This type of overinvolvement seems to be a continuation of a picture found in some families of schizophrenics even prior to the illness. In these families, each member experiences not just a feeling of competition with the others, but an extreme sense of participation, reactivity, and special sensitivity to the actions of the others, often interpreted in a negative way. The members of the family want to help each other, but because of their particular entanglements, anxiety, distrust, and misinterpretation, they end up by hurting one another. They remind one of some of Chekov's characters, whose personalities and intense involvement with one another lead gradually to an unfortunate outcome.

A morbid degree of overinvolvement, however, may not be so frequent as Wing and others seem to imply. Cultural differences may play a role. Wing and his colleagues have worked with patients and families who come almost exclusively from Anglo-Saxon backgrounds. What is considered overinvolvement in that milieu may be the usual state of affairs in Italian and Jewish families. In other words, in evaluating these factors, the ethnic background and the particular prevailing family culture must be considered.

Distortions and Their Avoidance

As we have already mentioned, the recovering patient may misinterpret what relatives say and may distort what goes on between him and the family, without even realizing that he has done so. This development takes place particularly frequently at a certain stage of recovery from the illness. When the patient returns to the family, he may have lost all his delusions or false beliefs that, by their very remoteness from reality, were easily recognized, even by laymen, as indications of illness. The patient now merely distorts. Distortions are based on reality, but the proportions or the various ingredients of the real situation are altered. These distortions may make humane involvement on the part of the family seem like morbid overinvolvement, intrusion, innuendos, insults. Although these distortions are treated with psychotherapy given by a professional, it is important to discuss them here for the sake of family members, so that they can recognize them and learn to prevent their occurrence.

A white lie told by a relative – for instance, 'How well you look in that dress' – is transformed by the patient into the worst mendacity. A word that should reveal only tactlessness is viewed as a symbol of falsity or perversion. As we have seen in Chapter 5, such deformations are caused by the patient's need to reproduce a pattern established in childhood, a pattern that was the result not only of what really happened but also of the patient's lack of knowledge, youthful immaturity, and misperception. Once the mother of a patient told her, 'Your mother-in-law is sick.' The patient interpreted her mother's words as if they meant, 'With your perverse qualities you have made your mother-in-law sick, as you made me sick once.' Another time the mother asked what the patient was making for dinner. The patient interpreted her mother's remarks as criticisms. Mother intimated that she was not a good cook and did not know how to plan a meal. On still another occasion the mother spoke about the beautiful apartment that the patient's newly married younger sister had just furnished. The patient – who, incidentally, was jealous of the mother's attention to her sister – intepreted this remark as meaning, 'Your sister has much better taste than you.'

Interpretations of this kind may indeed increase the anxiety of the patient and hasten a new psychotic episode. If the family members were not involved with the patient, these hurtful situations would not be likely to occur. However, distance is not desirable either and does not promote rehabilitation. If the patient undergoes psychotherapy, he will discuss these little incidents with the therapist and the atmosphere will be clarified. The family is not qualified to do this job; relatives may start to defend themselves unnecessarily and the little incident may degenerate into a furious verbal battle.

The therapist, on the other hand, because of his training, is able to explain to the patient why he has the need to follow a pattern and to reaffirm and maintain the old image that he had of the relative. Generally by reporting and analyzing with the therapist these little incidents of daily life, the patient comes to the realization that if his parents or the other important people in his life have negative traits, these traits are not necessarily arrows or weapons used purposely to hurt him. They are merely characteristics of these people that should not be considered prevailing qualities or features representative of their total personality. For instance, in the example above of the patient and her mother, we may indeed recognize some elements of hostility in the mother's remarks. As a matter of fact, one may think that the patient not only was *not* distorting but was very close to the truth, because she had become particularly sensitive to her mother's hostility – hostility that others wanted to deny. Such a situation is often reminiscent of a Pirandello drama, in which we do not know who is right and who is wrong. In this example, the therapist helped the patient to recognize that she may have been correct in her evaluation of some particular aspects of her mother's communication. Yes, there might have been more than an element of hostility in mother's remarks, elements of which the mother might not have been aware. But even in a very loving relationship some elements of hostility may persist, and we must assess them in their right proportion, without magnifying their import.

In every human relationship and communication, in every social event, there are many dimensions and meanings. The patient focuses on the negative parts and neglects all the other dimensions of a rich communication, which may include aspects of warmth and genuine concern. It is difficult for the patient to tolerate any ambivalence, any plurality of dimensions. Psychotherapy will help him to accept this plurality as inherent in human life.

The example above may give hints to family members, too, on how to improve relationships with the recovering patient. The family must learn to recognize and avoid the patient's areas of vulnerability, and this, of course, may not be easy. The mother knew that the patient felt some rivalry toward her sister, and that she did not feel competent as a housekeeper and a cook. She also knew that her daughter was interested only in a professional career. Why did she have to bring up these issues? And as far as the mother-in-law was concerned, why didn't the mother leave it up to the patient's husband to convey the news? All this indicates that the mother was somewhat insensitive, but not necessarily as malevolent or purposely destructive as the patient saw her to be. The mother's insensivity, in its turn, may have been the result of psychological circumstances that we cannot investigate here. As we already indicated, living with a recovering schizophrenic does require an increase in sensitivity on the part of the family members. The higher degree of sensitivity, if attained, will have many beneficial effects on the lives of all the members of the family.

We have already mentioned some of the contrasting, at times even opposite, positions that we have to take in dealing with a recovering schizophrenic, and we have stressed how difficult veering between these different directions is. We must mention a few more problems. One of them is the situation in which the patient's need both for companionship and for privacy is essential and must be satisfied. Time must be found for both. Another difficult balance must be made between the patient's need for freedom and for structure. The patient must experience freedom of action; yet a structure, a routine, a schedule should be worked out with him, at least for the first few months after his return from the hospital. Although structured, his day should not become packed with things to do or be too complex. The level of complexity has to be adjusted to the patient's capability.

The home is almost always unable to provide for all the needs of a person who, although convalescing, is not yet capable of resuming his usual activities. As we shall see in Chapter 9, it may be desirable for the patient to spend some time in day hospitals or clubs for former patients. The aid of a psychiatric companion, nurse, or therapeutic assistant is advisable only for patients who do not recover or are not even greatly improved, as we shall discuss in Chapter 10.

If the patient maintains some links with the hospital from which he was discharged, these links are generally handled through the offices of a social worker. The position of the social worker has changed, too, in the new milieu of rehabilitation of the recovering schizophrenic. Whereas in the 1950s and 1960s the social worker was requested by the hospital or by the psychiatrist in charge to make an accurate inquiry into how much the family contributed to the patient's condition, now he is instructed to search for all those positive family attributes and facilities that the patient can use for his rehabilitation. He can assume an active role in organizing a program for the patient.

Important Events and Important Decisions

At times the family is confronted by unusual happenings in the life of the patient. Although these events are usually discussed at length with the therapist, the family may become involved even before the therapist or there may be no therapist to turn to. The patient has become acquainted with a person of the opposite sex (or, more seldom, of the same sex) and wants to go to live with him or her. In other cases, the patient may want to become engaged or get married right away. The family has the strong feeling that the patient is not ready and yet does not want to exert pressure to such an extent as to make him feel restrained or unduly controlled. The delaying technique – trying to persuade the patient to wait for a time when he feels more at ease with the programs that are formulated – is the proper response. However, if the patient insists and cannot be persuaded to postpone his plans, the best thing is to go along with him and be of as much help as possible. An attitude of open revolt, opposition, or retaliation is not advisable and may be counterproductive.

The same thing could be repeated for the recovering schizophrenic who wants to become pregnant. Pregnancy and motherhood are real challenges for all women. To deliberately cause such a complication while the patient is recovering is not recommendable. Lest I be misunderstood, I want to clarify the point. I do not say that recovering schizophrenics or former schizophrenics should not become mothers. Some are excellent mothers. However, for many patients – even those with the best results – there is a period of time (at least a year to as much as five years) during which some difficulty remains in coping with unusual and demanding challenges like pregnancy, childbirth, and motherhood. If the patient is under drug therapy, she must be even more careful not to become pregnant, because the safety of most drugs in pregnancy and lactation has not been established, although there is no evidence of fetal malformations. A certain amount of drug is secreted in human milk.

At times the patient wants to do something drastic, for instance, leave the spouse and the children. The spouse who is threatened with being left alone after going through the hardship of the illness and offering loyalty and support often feels mortified. At other times the spouse is ready to accept the decision, which often cannot be reversed. Again the delaying technique is best, but if the patient goes through with the plans, the family must be supportive. We must remember that the patient is not likely to break an important family relationship because of a whim or a capricious impulse, but only because of inability to cope with the circumstances. If children are involved, the best possible arangements must be made for their care. Although I have said that some former schizophrenics or even schizophrenics are excellent parents, it is also true that a recovering patient who feels unable to cope with the circumstances may be very disturbing to a young child. A substitute parent has to be found.

A question that comes up quite frequently is the following: Should the recovering patient be told the truth when some terrible event (sudden death or the diagnosis of a serious disease) occurs to a relative or other person dear to the patient? Over thirty years ago, when I was working in a state hospital, I was instructed by older psychiatrists to advise the family always to tell the truth. Certainly we do not want to lie to patients or anybody else. However, there is a good time and a bad time for telling the truth. State hospital psychiatrists used to insist that no ill effects have ever resulted from the revelation of bad news. They were referring to a group of patients who, in addition to being ill, often lived in a state of alienation aggravated by the environment. Many of these patients were not able to express their emotions. An apparent insensitivity should not be interpreted as imperviousness. Even a catatonic schizophrenic who seems insensitive and is immobile like a statue feels very strongly. A volcano of emotions is often disguised by his petrified appearance.

With the recovering schizophrenic we find ourselves in a completely different situation. He is very sensitive and would not forgive the relatives for not telling him the truth. And yet knowing the truth may be detrimental to him when he is still unstable and still struggling to recover fully his mental health. The patient has to be prepared gradually and eventually be told the truth when he has already anticipated in his own mind its possibility and the methods of coping with it.

Another question is how to counsel a recovering patient who asks about disclosing his illness to important people in his life. If he is engaged, should he tell his fiancée that he has been ill with schizophrenia? If he applies to a college, should he put on the application form that he has been hospitalized with a psychiatric disorder? Again, when I was a resident in psychiatry, I was instructed to advise the patient always to tell the truth. Certainly we wish the truth to be known and to prevail. A person who wants to accept another human being in the intimate relation of wife or husband must be willing to let that person know important things about his or her life and have a confident expectation about the result of the revelation. However, this is different from directing the patient to tell the truth. Nobody has the right to do that, neither the therapist nor the parents. It is up to the patient himself to choose and decide. It is also up to the others involved to decide how they will react to the news.

As far as writing about a past hospitalization on an application for college is concerned, I wish we could always advise the patient to tell the truth; but again it is too much of a responsibility to do so. Only the patient or the patient and his parents must decide together. This may seem strange to the reader, but I must report some unpleasant experiences I have had relating to this matter. I have treated some patients who, in applying to college, reported their past schizophrenic illness, or whose teachers or deans, in writing about them to admissions committees, reported the illness. In several cases, in spite of the fact that these students were completely recovered and had an excellent academic record, they had difficulty being accepted at some colleges. Despite assertions to the contrary, some admissions committees in colleges and graduate schools retain prejudices toward mental illness. I must say in fairness that this prejudice is rapidly decreasing, and that some of my patients have been admitted to the best colleges in spite of their previous illness, which was fully reported. Good colleges, oriented toward the new developments of medicine and provided with a psychologically sophisticated staff, do not have prejudices of this sort. But at times it is difficult to ascertain which attitude prevails at a given college.

Concluding Remarks

In summary, living with a recovering schizophrenic is a hard task, but not an insurmountable one. It can be rewarding not only for the patient but for everyone concerned. If we compare the hardship of living with a recovering or partially recovered schizophrenic with that of living with a severe alcoholic, a blind person, an epileptic, or a person chronically ill with some incapacitating disease, living with a recovering schizophrenic is considerably easier. An atmosphere of hope prevails in many cases, and the satisfaction of seeing results at least partially due to the family's cooperative efforts confers a joyful climate of further expectation. Even in a family with young children, although the situation is further complicated, the task is not necessarily an impossible one. If the children are big enough to understand, they should be told that a member of the family is ill and requires special regard. Some of the unusual attitudes of the ill person should be explained to the children in terms of illness and in a context of serious but hopeful concern. Children generally respond well to adverse or abnormal conditions provided there are compensating circumstances. In the midst of an atmosphere of warm care and frank discussion, the presence of a mental illness in a member of the family tends to remain a smaller part of the child's life than is generally assumed, and in some cases a part that promotes maturation.

9. The Outcome: Clinical Pictures, Management, Care

Predictability of the Outcome

As we mentioned in Chapter 1, the outcome of schizophrenia ranges from complete recovery to chronic aggravation of the condition.

We must stress that the number of good outcomes is increasing and that with future improvements in methods of treatment the percentage of complete recoveries will become even higher.

The Finnish authors Niskanen and Achté are among those who have done the most important statistical work on the outcome of cases of schizophrenia, studying patients who were admitted to hospitals in 1950, 1960, and 1965. The percentage of patients who recovered completely or were socially recovered after a period of five years was 59 percent of the patients in 1950, 68 percent in 1960, and 64 percent in 1965. The findings also suggested that the proportion of those who were in need of hospital treatment after a period of five years decreased steadily: 22 percent of the 1950 patients; 14 percent of the 1960 patients; and 10 percent of the 1965 patients.

These findings are indeed encouraging. We can confirm that patients who recover or become capable of more or less adequate social life constitute approximately two-thirds of the original schizophrenic population.

In the past, before the introduction of the major modern methods of treatment, the prognosis or prediction of the outcome of a case of schizophrenia was based purely on the characteristics of the initial symptomatology and the course of the illness. The emphasis now is on influencing the course of schizophrenia rather than on relying exclusively on the benevolent aspect of the initial symptoms.

Nevertheless, there is still merit in evaluating the symptomatology. Among the most important favorable characteristics are the following:

1. The more acute the beginning, the more favorable the outcome. This criterion is reliable in a majority of cases, but not in all.

2. If the occurrence of an obvious specific precipitating factor, like loss of employment, a broken engagement, or childbirth, forms a prominent part of the complex cause of schizophrenia, the person has a relatively better chance of reintegrating once this factor is removed or no longer operating.

3. Conscious anxiety is an important indication of favorable outcome. Its presence indicates that a prognostically unfavorable blunting of affect has not eliminated this emotion, even at a conscious level. Because it is distressing, anxiety stimulates the patient to continue his search and possibly to return to reality.

4. A stormy type of personality indicates a more favorable outcome.

5. A general attitude of compliance towards therapists and nurses is a favorable characteristic. This criterion is particularly reliable in paranoids.

6. The ability to pretend or to lie is a good prognostic sign. Delusional life is reality for a patient, not pretension. In severe cases, when questioned about his delusions the patient cannot deny them or lie about their existence because he cannot shift to an imaginary assumption. The denial of delusions that are real to him requires the power to abstract or to shift to a set of facts that, from his point of view, are unreal. When the patient is able to lie about his delusions, he is in the process of recovery. He won't have to lie for very long because the delusions will soon disappear. (We must remember that schizophrenics treated with even moderate amounts of tranquilizers often reacquire the ability to lie. This criterion then does not apply to them.)

Adverse prognostic features in a considerable number of cases – but not in all – are the following:

1. Slow, insidious beginning of the illness.

2. Absence of precipitating factors or easily ascertainable psychological causes.

3. Blunting of affect and marked schizoid type of personality.

4. General attitude of defiance towards doctors and nurses.

5. Attempt to blame others and exonerate oneself. This criterion is not always valid.

6. Acceptance of one's illness or resignation to being sick. This trait belongs more properly to advanced stages of schizophrenia.

In what follows we shall take into consideration three groups of patients:

1. Those who have entirely overcome the illness.
2. Those who remain moderately ill.
3. Those who are chronically ill.

We shall describe these three conditions and outline long-range plans for those in the second and third groups.

Patients Who Overcome Schizophrenia

Yes, schizophrenia is curable. People get well and completely recover, in spite of the pessimistic attitudes of the past. However, only about one-third recover. We must also clarify what we mean by 'cured.' We have already mentioned that, although loss of all symptoms is one good outcome, it is not the best of all desirable results in psychiatry. Traditional medicine considers a cure a return to the state that existed prior to the onset of the illness. But a psychiatrist cannot be satisfied with a return to a type of personality that had many weaknesses and was vulnerable to attacks of mental disease. He strives for more. He wants the patient to acquire the capacity for establishing good relationships with other human beings, closeness with a few persons, love for a spouse and children. The patient must have reorganized his personality in such a way that now he has a sense of identity. He knows who he is, and he accepts himself; he even likes himself. He has a sense of purpose and hope; he believes in the possibility of his own fulfillment. In other words, he must see himself, life, the world, and the future in a different way.

It is possible to obtain such results in a considerable percentage of cases. Many former patients have stated that the illness was a helpful experience for them, something they had to go through in order to become able to face life without fear and with fewer conflicts, less hesitation, and greater ability to confront difficulties and cope with them. They feel as if they are born into a new life. During the illness they sometimes believed, in a delusional way and in an attempt to escape from their lives, that they were *literally* reborn. Now they feel as if they were reborn because they recognize in themselves capacities they never dreamed of being able to acquire. We psychiatrists do not go as far as some former patients in thinking that it is a good thing to go through a schizophrenic experience. It is not something we would recommend. We prefer to avert schizophrenia whenever we can because we can never be sure that the results will be good. But it is beyond doubt that, as a result of satisfactory treatment, which includes psychotherapy, many patients achieve a degree of maturity far superior to the one that existed prior to the illness.

If, however, by cure we mean achieving a state of immunity, with no possibility of recurrence later in life, then we are not yet in a position to make definite statements. Statistics are still controversial, and the methods applied do not lend themselves to comparison. However, we can affirm that if treatment succeeds in altering the fundamental psychological patterns and is able to effect a basic reorganization of the personality, a recurrence is much less likely to occur.

At a practical level, successfully treated patients learn to deal with the challenges of life. They also learn to recognize what they cannot cope with and how to avoid it. Finally, they learn to recognize and avoid the particular type of anxiety that does not abate but intensifies.

In reviewing cases treated satisfactorily with methods that included intense psychotherapy, I came to the conclusion that my optimistic predictions proved to be accurate in a large majority of cases. However, a few patients treated to a degree that was deemed satisfactory nevertheless had relapses. They remained vulnerable to fear-provoking situations. It is important to add that in most of these cases the relapses were moderate in intensity and the patients recovered.

Recurrence of schizophrenic attacks is evaluated differently today from the way it was before the major types of treatment – especially intensive psychodynamically oriented psychotherapy – came into existence. In the past, the third attack (or hospitalization) was considered crucial. The third episode meant that the patient was moving irretrievably toward chronic schizophrenia. In patients who have been adequately treated, second or third attacks are generally milder than the previous ones and are of shorter duration. By no means do they indicate an unfavorable ultimate outcome, and the patient and his family should be so reassured. It is only when one attack is more serious than the previous one that a favorable outcome is in serious doubt. Many psychiatrists have seen former patients achieve a very satisfactory style of life. Some have obtained important positions in the business world, in the arts, in academic life, and in other spheres.

If I were to look for a common negative characteristic in patients whom I have successfully treated, I would say that quite a number of them have married persons intellectually inferior to them. The common positive quality that stands out is that eventually they were able to find love in life, although to varying degrees.

This statement does not imply that all the troubles of the patient are over after successful therapy. In the famous words of Frieda Fromm-Reichmann, we cannot promise a rose garden. It would be unrealistic to believe that the promise of life is a promise comparable to a garden, Utopian for the patient and Utopian for us. But it is realistic to promise the patient what we promise ourselves – that sooner or later we will have our own little garden.

Patients Who Remain Moderately Ill

The picture is not always so rosy. We have already mentioned that in 30 to 40 percent of patients, treatment attains only partial goals.

Several situations may result. Some patients, although still presenting signs of the illness, are capable of making a better adjustment than the one they had before they became ill. Some disclose more definite signs of the illness, and we cannot even say that they have reached a level of adjustment similar to the one prevailing before the onset of the illness.

An atmosphere of pessimism should not overshadow other considerations in these cases. In some of them a slow improvement may go on for several years. At times the improvement is so slow as to be almost imperceptible, but when we evaluate the condition of the patient after long periods of time, we see satisfactory progress. This development reminds me of stop-motion photography. When the growth of plants and the blossoming of flowers is photographed at normal speed, we see only a static representation. Nothing seems to change. But in stop-motion photography, the plant is photographed at intervals that are made into a coherent film, and we can see the growth, unfolding, and blossoming of the plant by viewing the plant at different moments over a long period of its existence.

If the patient lives with his family, the procedures described in Chapter 8 should be adopted. In many other cases some outside facilities must be resorted to. They will be described in the next section of this chapter.

The picture presented by those patients who remain at an intermediary stage are many and quite different. In a few instances we see a patient who shows an excess of life and zest, just as some normal persons do. Most of the time, however, we see a person who lacks spontaneity, wholeheartedness, a sense of commitment, a desire to participate and to share. He cannot be a self-starter. He requires constant stimulation; yet unless this coaxing is done with great tact and gentleness, it may do him more harm than good. When he has to focus his thoughts upon a certain subject, the patient shows inability to concentrate and gives only a tepid and blurred response. Other patients maintain an overriding suspiciousness. They continue to interpret everything as being done purposely against them. On rare occasions they may hear imaginary voices and express bizarre ideas, although by no means as frequently as during the acute episode. Some of them gradually tend to reduce their lives to a routine and, unless helped with perseverance, they live an impoverished life.

Two basic goals become the guidelines for patients who remain moderately ill.

1. Make sure the patient continues the treatment given during the beginning of the illness. The treatment, to be given by professionals, consists of the same procedures described in Chapter 6, with some modifications.

2. Arrange for rehabilitation and restoration of the patient to his old environment or to a new environment, taking into account that he may or may not lose some of the handicaps caused by the illness.

We can formulate our goals in a different way:

1. The restoration of mental health.
2. The ability to live a satisfactory life in spite of the residue of the illness.

Some rules of thumb may be useful in dealing with partially recovered patients.

1. First of all, we must accept that, at least for a certain period of time, the patient cannot live a life as intense as we would like. We have to accept his present limitations. To force him to do what he cannot do would be risking arousal of great anxiety and worsening of his general condition. We have to move toward him more than we expect him to move toward us. We must keep in mind that any project of rehabilitation is a long procedure and not a frontal attack.

2. The patient should not be treated as a person who is irresponsible or likely to harm himself or others. Statistics have never proved that violence or criminal behavior is more frequent in schizophrenics than in the general population.

3. Although the patient is not totally in touch with reality, he is still capable to a large extent of assessing life correctly. He is not a mental defective. He should not be treated as a child, or as an inferior person, or as an object. We must always respect his human dignity. We must inspire trust and hope. We should not assail him with questions like, 'Why did you do that?' or 'Why did you say that?' or 'Why don't you talk?' We should not say anything that will make him feel accused, depreciated, rejected, or on trial.

4. Although the patient seems insensible and detached from the world, we must remember that he is affected by his environment even when no response is visible. It is because he is so sensitive that often he puts up this armor of detachment.

5. When schizophrenic patients are provoked excessively, or treated cruelly, or requested to do what they cannot do they are likely to become aggressive. However, when they express delusional ideas of being disparaged, ridiculed, or persecuted, this behavior should be brought up with the psychiatrist in charge, not a paraprofessional.

6. Even though the patient shows signs or traces of mental illness, a major part of his psyche remains healthy. We must appeal to this healthy part. We must clarify and explain, but not more than he can absorb. We must not be reluctant to explain the same thing time and time again.

Subsequent interrelationships with patients who have reached an intermediary stage between health and illness must be adjusted to their specific and individual needs. The general climate must be one similar to that described in Chapter 8. The patients must know they can expect to get better. They must at the same time do their best to adhere to a program or a plan that has been specifically designed for them.

If, in spite of all these general measures, the patient regresses and displays childlike behavior or indulges in uncontrollable fits of rage, screaming, and crying, we must conclude that the family environment is not the best place for his rehabilitation.

A considerable number of professionals believe that if the patient remains moderately ill, no rehabilitation should be attempted in the family environment. I want to stress that this point of view is not unanimously upheld. We often encounter another set of facts: The family would like to participate fully in the rehabilitation of the patient, but special conditions (the presence of children, pregnant women, invalids, great hostility and resentment for the patient, extreme sensitivity or emotional instability of some family members) make it vital that the rehabilitation takes place outside the family immediately after the patient's discharge from the hospital.

Fortunately many organizations exist for the rehabilitation of the moderately ill schizophrenic, and the number of patients who make use of them is rapidly increasing. Lengthy hospitalization, even for patients who remain sick to more than a moderate degree, is not recommended for several reasons. In many cases it leads to what has been called *institutionalitis* or *institutional neurosis* or *psychosis*, characterized by loss of individuality, resignation, apathy, and withdrawal.

Clinical and rehabilitation facilities are available in many psychiatric hospitals, too. They remain, however, in the sheltered hospital environment, and the way the patient adjusts to them is not a sure indication of how he will manage later in the facilities offered by the community, which will permit him to be in closer contact with the hazards of life.

The tendency today is towards forms of rehabilitation offered by the community, with the understood premise that, after a period of community-organized rehabilitation, the patient will again be the concern of the family. Then those recommendations and procedures described in Chapter 8 will have to be followed. We must stress again that the aim should not be a final assignment of the patient to an organization that would replace the old state hospital. The final goal is a return of the patient to his family, or to a new family. Only when it will not be possible to achieve these goals because of the advanced age of the patient, or because there is no family, should other arrangements be considered final goals.

If by *community reintegration* or *return to the community* we mean becoming part of the general population of the community immediately after discharge from the hospital, and without the use of these specific agencies, then we must realize that we use euphemisms. We use nostalgic or desirable terms based on social conditions that do not exist. Living outside hospitals in some populated areas does not necessarily mean becoming a member of the community. Traditional communities – where people knew each other and had established common interests, concerns, and support – are rare today even for normal people because of industrialization, the formation of big urban centers, and the mobility of the population.

Rehabilitation Centers in the Community

Historical Background

In 1955 a Joint Commission on Mental Illness and Health stated that 'Experience with certain community outpatient clinics and rehabilitation centers would seem to indicate that many mental patients could be better treated on an outpatient basis at much lower cost than by a hospital.' The Joint Commission's 1961 final report, *Action for Mental Health*, suggested that psychiatric hospitals be reduced in size, increase their resources, and extend their services to the community. The commission recommended returning the patient to home and community life as soon as possible and keeping him there with the help of 'day hospitals, night hospitals, aftercare clinics, public health nursing services, foster family care, convalescent nursing homes, rehabilitation centers, work services and expatient groups . . . so long as they are soundly conceived, well staffed, and operated as part of an integrated system of mental patient services.'

In 1963 President Kennedy, in the first message about mental illness sent to Congress by a president of the United States, advocated a new approach to mental illness in which 'the cold way' of the old methods of hospitalization would be replaced 'by the open warmth of community concern and capability.' This new attitude was too optimistic for a certain category of patients – those who remain seriously and chronically ill. We shall discuss their situation later in this chapter. However, for patients who remain moderately ill, the approach signaled a new era and opened up new possibilities.*

Early Transitional Stages:
Night and Day Hospitals

When patients leave the protective environment of the hospital and are not advised to return to their own families, they must go

---

*Similar developments took place during the same period in other countries throughout the world, including the United Kingdom.

through different transitional stages of rehabilitation. For some of them the first step is the *night hospital*. Some patients feel particularly anxious at night, either because they are afraid of danger in the environment, which they feel is increased at night, or because they are afraid of themselves, that is, of giving vent to impulses and symptoms when night comes.

The *day hospital* goes one step further. It is particularly valuable insofar as it can easily replace the full hospital, and it can also offer excellent programs of rehabilitation.

The first psychiatric day hospital was organized by M. A. Dzhagarov in Russia in 1933, but the project remained unknown to Western countries for several years. The first one on the American continent was organized in 1947 in Montreal by Ewen Cameron, and one was begun by Joshua Bierer in 1948 in England. Day hospitals grew rapidly in the United States, especially after 1963 when, in order to qualify for federal funds, each community mental health center had to have a day-care facility. Whereas in the United States there were only 37 day hospitals in 1960, there were 149 by March 1964. Their number has since progressively increased. The patient suitable for a day hospital must not be so disturbed as to be too difficult for the family to manage at night, and he must be able to travel back and forth to the hospital.

Day hospitals have many advantages. They are less expensive than full hospitals. Dormitories do not need to be built. Staffing costs are cut by the elimination of two of the three shifts of workers, and by the reduction from a seven-day to a five-day operation. Some traditional procedures of full-time hospitals are no longer necessary. To test the patient's reaction to his usual environment, it is no longer necessary to send him home for half-days or on weekends. The patient does not feel confined to a total institution. He does not feel 'crazy' any more, or behind locked doors, or separated from the rest of the world. He retains enough ties with the family and his social environment, yet these ties are not strong enough to bring about conflicts and disturbances. The day hospital eliminates sharp discontinuity between family and full-time hospitals and vice versa, which at times used to bring about unpleasant results. The day hospital, of course, offers those facilities (described in Chapter 7) that full hospitals have.

I have so far described the day hospital as a transitional stage from full hospital to family environment. But the reverse is also appropriate in many cases. Many patients may go directly to the day hospital without ever going to a full hospital. This is a frequent occurrence when the patient continues to receive regular office treatment from his own psychiatrist.

In the minds of many persons the psychiatric day hospital is not as a rule connected with old-fashioned ideas about mental illness. Many patients who resist the idea of going to a regular psychiatric hospital have little or no objection to going to a day hospital. The family, too, generally accepts this arrangement easily. The term *day center* seems a more appropriate name than *day hospital* and should be more commonly used.

Halfway Houses and Similar Facilities

Halfway houses are residential centers organized to meet the needs of patients who are halfway between the condition they had in the hospital and full rehabilitation. The expression *halfway* should not be taken literally. Many patients have progressed more than halfway, some less. Some halfway houses are also equipped as day centers. Residents of halfway houses that are not so equipped can go to a regular day center during the day.

The most common type of halfway house is a former boarding house or an old house donated by philanthropists. Many halfway houses establish a maximum period of time (from sixty days to a year) during which the resident can stay, but in most places these time limits are not rigidly enforced. The policy of time limitation not only gives many people the benefit of the halfway house but it also reminds them that this is not a permanent arrangement. They must work toward their reintegration in the community.

Generally halfway houses are nonprofit institutions. Some do not charge any fees whatsoever; some are quite expensive. The staff members have permanent positions and are trained to handle the psychological problems of the residents, at least at a practical-behavioral level. Social workers and volunteers may be part of the staff. The residents must maintain a certain discipline and must respect rules. The discipline is not harsh, however, and infractions are generally discussed by residents before disciplinary actions are taken. Residents are given rotating functions within the organization.

Although a general climate of friendliness and acceptance is characteristic of all halfway houses, their general policy varies. Thus, the one most appropriate for the particular needs of the patient must be selected. Some halfway houses are called *high-expectation centers*. There the patients must attend classes or work or both. In others the expectation is intermediate. In all types of halfway houses, extreme permissiveness is discouraged lest the atmosphere become that of an institution for the chronically ill where regressive features, passivity, and self-neglect are not combated. High-expectation halfway houses are said to yield better results than low-expectation halfway houses. However, it is hard to say how much this difference is based on the original selection of residents.

Unfortunately there are not enough halfway houses, especially in some parts of the country, to provide for the great need. These institutions offer their services to patients with psychiatric conditions other than schizophrenia. However, alcoholics, drug addicts, fetishists, exhibitionists, and transvestites are excluded. Some halfway houses are organized for prolonged residence and include definite work possibilities. Some are in a rural environment and can be called ranches and farms.

Dr Israel Zwerling, a psychiatrist who has done much research on the care of psychiatric patients after hospitalization, values first the establishment of small patient groups in the course of hospital treatment, and second the discharge of these patients as a unit to a residence in the community. This is how he described the care that Dr Fairweather and his associates are offering at the Palo Alto Veterans Administration Hospital.

They [Dr Fairweather's staff] studied a group of seventy-five chronic patients who were moved into a motel (the 'Lodge') after a four-week planning period in the hospital devoted to discussing the problems they would face in the community and the possible solutions to these problems. Except for an occasional visit by a staff member on a specific mission, the Lodge was completely organized and operated by the patients. Jobs... in the community were taken by Lodge units rather than by individual patients; the work responsibility of a patient indisposed and incapable of working for a brief period could then be assumed by other Lodge members, so that the job would not be lost. The living and working arrangements, such as who would do the marketing, the cooking, the bookkeeping, etc., essential for maintaining the Lodge, and who would cover which outside jobs, were established by group meetings of Lodge residents. The results were extremely impressive: in the first six months, 63 percent of the Lodge group remained out of the hospital and 50 percent were employed full-time during this period; in contrast, in a carefully matched control group, 24 percent remained out of the hospital and only 3 percent worked for the full six-month period. The differences between the two groups remained strikingly significant over the thirty-month follow-up period. What is of greatest interest is that there were no significant differences in symptoms between the two groups when the patients were studied individually; the symptoms ceased to be disabling in the setting of the Lodge. The social structure of the Lodge permitted the evolution of an extremely effective system of mutual supports in which the disability of any one patient, which might have rendered him incapable of coping in the community if he were living alone, could be made up for by others in the group.

There are organizations offering rehabilitation that are difficult to define because they have some characteristics of day centers, some of halfway houses, and some of clubs of former patients. Fountain House in New York City was the first to be organized and is probably still the best known.

Fountain House as an organization was founded by patients from Rockland State Hospital in the early 1940s. In 1948 funds were raised to buy a brownstone house in mid-Manhattan. In the 1950s a daytime program was added under the directorship of John Beard. Fountain House aims at helping its residents to reestablish a sense of belonging and of being needed. It tries to create a new and extended family that has attitudes toward friendship, working together, and helping one another that are different from the usual ones.

The following words of the director, John Beard, as reported in a study published by the Joint Information Service of the American Psychiatric Association and the National Association for Mental Health, are eloquent and illustrative.

People want to feel significant, and to do so they must get into a setting whose purpose is conducive to feeling significant. Because we are working with clients who are 'the least promising,' our staff feel that any success or accomplishment is significant. Take our restaurant project. We have very sick, vocationally disabled members there, seventeen of them, and they are working, earning real salaries, in a real place of business that is making a profit. The staff can respond to this kind of success.

If we took even the very best, most highly recovered member we have ever had at Fountain House and presented him for examination to a psychiatric resident, if that resident were competent he would still make a diagnosis of schizophrenia. But that's not relevant because the member is functioning in society. The diagnosis becomes just academic. So my persuasion is that the reason schizophrenics in the community are in such bad shape is [that] we've failed to give them the kinds of experiences that will maximize their ego function.

Beard added that the staff of Fountain House is not interested in the patient's sickness *per se* or in his background, but rather in teaching the patients 'what they need to know and giving them the supports they have to have to work and to live in the community and have a decent kind of life.'

At the time the above report was written (1971), Fountain House had fifty-six full-time and ten part-time staff members. When the present Fountain House was built, across the street from the original brownstone on 47th Street, the cost of the building was approximately $2 million. Over 80 percent of its members were once diagnosed as schizophrenic. More than 300 persons participate each day in the daytime activities, and many more attend the evening and weekend programs. The social program includes many opportunities for listening to music, playing a variety of games, and watching television together. The activities, most of which take place in the evening and on weekends, include dramatics, photography, swimming, basketball, trips to movies, group discussions, and outings.

The vocational program is the most impressive part of the Fountain House activities, aiming at preparing patients for work and finding occupations for them. It is divided into two stages:

1. Prevocational activities carried out within the Fountain House setting. Members work in the reception office, thrift shop,

snack bar, dining room, at educational activities, and so on.

2. Placements in a large number of New York City businesses and stores. Even such major firms as Sears, Roebuck, *Newsweek* magazine, and the largest banks have participated in the program and have offered 'transitional jobs' to members of Fountain House.

Other important rehabilitation centers are Horizon House in Philadelphia, Council House in Pittsburgh, Threshholds in Chicago, Portal House in Los Angeles, and Hill House in Cleveland.

Occupational Rehabilitation and Former-Patient Clubs

In addition to those connected with halfway houses and rehabilitation centers, other programs for occupational rehabilitation are provided elsewhere and it is hoped that more and more will be established. C H I R P (Community Hospital Industry Rehabilitation Program) is connected with the Brockton, Massachusetts Veterans Administration. Patients are paid for the work they do while attending educational and manual arts therapies.

The 141 workshops of the national programs under the aegis of Goodwill Industries accept people with psychiatric histories. The Altro workshops, part of the Rehabilitation Center for Chronic Relapsing Illnesses, admit psychiatric patients also. The National Association of Sheltered Workshops consists of 1,300 workshops, approximately a thousand of which accept people with psychiatric diagnoses.

Of the several clubs that organize programs similar to those of some rehabilitation centers, the largest is Recovery, Incorporated, which was founded in 1937 and now has a membership of about 5,000.

Facilities such as those described above in the United States may also be found in the United Kingdom. The development of such facilities, however, has not paralleled the recent policy of increased discharge from hospital. The community services have failed to keep up with the continually increasing numbers of patients in the community. Thus many of the halfway house type of facility have been established by voluntary organizations rather than by the National Health Service. However, many Area Health

Authorities in association with Social Services Departments have established hostels and halfway houses for the rehabilitation of psychiatric patients. Dr Douglas Bennett of the Maudsley Hospital in London is establishing a District Services Center, in which he hopes to provide comprehensive psychiatric care for the community in which the hospital is found. This facility will include halfway houses, hostels with trained staff and bed-sitting accommodation with the minimum of supervision. It is hoped that patients will move progressively through these facilities, slowly equipping them for their reintroduction into normal life in the community. Unfortunately, such schemes are by no means common.

The Chronically and Seriously Ill

We must now tackle the most disturbing topic of this book, the problem of patients who not only do not recover from schizophrenia but continue to be chronically and seriously ill. If the reader of this book is a person who has been diagnosed in the distant past or even recently as suffering from schizophrenia, he cannot include himself in the group of people which we are going to discuss now. If he were one of them, he would not have been able to read this book or go beyond the first two or three pages. Thus, what is written in this section *does not apply to him.*

There is one pleasing consideration to be made even when we discuss this group of patients, and that is that they are decreasing in number. Furthermore, even within this group of very sick people, the most serious stages are much less frequently reached.

None of these patients is able to sustain a prolonged intellectual effort. Among the sickest we include a variety of clinical pictures. Some continue to be agitated, aggressive, and destructive and to talk in a loud way, answering imaginary voices. Paranoid ideations may remain well established, as in earlier stages. In the majority of such patients, however, hallucinations and delusions have disappeared or cannot be discovered. In some cases they are still present, but they are completely disorganized and deprived of emotional charge. The patients present a severe disorganization of thought processes, to the point that their ideas are understood only with great difficulty. Some patients have peculiar habits, characteristics of advanced levels of disintegration. Some of them collect a number of objects, generally of limited size and no practical use. They put them into bundles that they seem to value very much and keep as if they were precious possessions.

In a study I made many years ago of patients kept in wards for regressed and chronic cases, I found that some patients had hoarded and wrapped in bundles such things as papers of any kind – old letters, toilet paper, newspapers – pieces of wood, stones, leaves, sticks, soap, spoons, string, rags, hairpins, old toothbrushes, wire, cups, feathers, fruit cores, stale food, hair, pencils, pens, combs, small boxes, cardboard, and other things. We should not believe that only patients who have spent many years in hospitals or in old mental institutions have these habits. Occasionally we see patients of this type discharged from hospitals, and a few who have never been in hospitals, walking in the streets of cities and carrying the entire collection of objects with them as if it were an important part of their person. Less regressed patients who have developed this habit more recently may collect objects that have some symbolic or actual use – letters, pictures, recent newspapers. However, at a later stage they collect these things not in order to use them, but just for the sake of collecting them. Not only do they not use these objects, but they also start to hoard other useless objects.

This hoarding habit, although bizarre, has a meaning. The useless objects that the patient collects are useful to him. They represent the last vestiges of his relationships with people and things; they replace the important relationships he once had or dreamed of having; they maintain some tie with the external world. It is not advisable to deprive a patient of his bundles unless their excessive number and size make it impossible to keep them in the room assigned to him.

Other patients, particularly women, develop the habit of decorating themselves in unusual, conspicuous, and – in the eyes of the world – bizarre ways. They make excessive use of lipstick and eye shadow and may paint a large part of their faces. Some patients make bracelets, rings, or necklaces out of pieces of paper and rags. Many patients of both sexes adorn themselves by placing buttons, stamps, small boxes, corks, or coins on their chests. These habits must be interpreted as needs for activity, last attempts to do things that, to the regressed mind, appear as ways to improve oneself.

Patients who reach even more advanced stages of the illness become incontinent, do not dress themselves, and cannot take care of their personal needs. Their lives consist of either extreme passivity or impulsive, reflexlike behavior. Some of them have a tendency to put objects in their mouths and attempt to eat them whether they are edible or not.

I repeat that patients reaching these most advanced stages are very few today. If we visit the back wards of present-day psychiatric institutions, which are reserved for this type of patient, we can ascertain that most of these patients have been sick for a long time; some were admitted when modern types of treatment did not exist.

Drug therapy has succeeded in eliminating the screaming, violent, aggressive behavior of patients, but it has been less effective in eliminating these regressive features and primitive habits.

The problem is, what can we do for these seriously and chronically ill patients? Since they cannot return to normal life, what can be done to make their lives as comfortable and rewarding as possible? What can we do to help them not to be a serious hindrance to the lives of others? There are several possibilities, all of which, for one reason or another, are more or less unsatisfactory. We shall examine them separately, but briefly they are:

1. Return to family life
2. Psychiatric treatment
3. Permanent institutionalization
4. Respect of human rights
5. Reintegration into the community

In the group of patients we are now considering, there are many pictures of disintegration, some of which lend themselves better than others to a particular disposition.

Return to Family Life

The return to family life of severely ill patients is much more difficult than that of the moderately ill. First of all, the burden is much heavier, since the patient often has to be supervised for even his basic needs. Second, the relatives often feel that embarking upon such an arduous task is a lost cause and a questionable mission. A feeling of futility prevails, and whatever initial enthusiasm exists seems progressively to fade away. However, if the manifestations of the illness are confined to inactivity and incoherence without episodes of aggressive behavior, an inner reward may be experienced in caring for the seriously ill at home. I have seen quite a considerable number of patients kept at home by aging parents and treated with love and tenderness. Spouses and siblings are less willing to assume the burden.

Although keeping this type of patient at home is one of the most difficult projects to implement, it is the best and most desirable of all from the point of view of the patient. It is humane. How touching it is to see these patients treated with warmth and affection in their homes. This happens more frequently in villages and small towns, where life is less complicated. As a rule of thumb, we must stress that it is much more difficult to keep a very regressed schizophrenic at home than a senile or mentally defective person.

Psychiatric Treatment

Psychiatric treatment for severely ill patients yields limited results. Nevertheless, it is important for the patient to visit a psychiatrist at regular intervals for possible changes in medication and for general counseling about life conditions. Only a few psychiatrists do psychotherapy with this group of patients. In many of these cases the therapist's fee is paid by medicaid or medicare. Some clinics are connected with the hospital from which the patient was discharged; other clinics see patients with no personal income or family support for a nominal fee.

Permanent Institutionalization

A great deal has been written against big institutions such as state hospitals and provincial hospitals for the chronically and severely mentally ill. They have been compared to prisons or to places where only custodial care is given. We have to distinguish how much is true in these statements, how much is completely inaccurate, and how much is an exaggeration. In 1948 Albert Deutsch wrote *The Shame of the States*, in which he made an exposé of state hospitals. Some authors would like to see all patients discharged from state hospitals and relocated in other places like general hospitals, nursing homes, or new institutions. In some European countries new government rules require the closing of public mental institutions as soon as possible.

Some authors have shown that hospital life tends to make the psychiatric condition more chronic; that is, it perpetuates the symptoms. Traditional institutional life is unsatisfactory and would have an adverse effect even on normal persons. Outstanding among these authors is Erving Goffman,* who has reported in detail the conditions, experiences, and behavior of the chronically mentally ill in traditional institutions and dramatically portrayed the process of mortification that the patient undergoes there. According to Goffman, the hospital disrupts those actions that give the person the feeling that he has some command over his personal world and consequently the feeling of a sense of self. He cannot indulge in those actions that confer autonomy and initiative.

Many descriptions of mental institutions were made a considerable number of years ago when institutionalized psychiatric patients continued to increase in number every year, and when the institutions were still organized according to principles formulated in an earlier time when there was no effective treatment for mental illness. Many years ago it was a fact—no matter how unpleasant—that for the majority of patients the hospital could not offer anything but custodial care. It is true, however, that even the custodial care could have been much better, and that attempts should have been made to change the custodial institution into a therapeutic community. On the other hand, the new points of view about therapeutic milieu therapy had not been tried and the moral treatment of previous times had been forgotten. Furthermore, the

* E. Goffman, *Asylums. Essays on the Social Situation of Mental Patients and Other Inmates* (Garden City, N.Y.: Doubleday, 1961).

governments of some states, still under the influence of the years of the Depression, recommended the strictest economy in the management of state hospitals.

The situation has fortunately changed to a considerable extent and is still in the process of changing for the better. First of all, the number of patients in state and county psychiatric hospitals, which in 1955 had reached a peak of 558,922, was by 1976 lowered to 193,436, a reduction of 65.4 percent, despite a pronounced increase in the total population of the United States. Second, 30 to 40 percent of these are patients readmitted for recurring episodes. The new policy recommends discharging patients as soon as possible and being less concerned with the uncertainty of the outcome. Third, another big percentage is made up of new admissions. If the bulk of patients consists of new admissions and short readmissions, the hospital is no longer a place for custodial care. It is true, however, that a hard core of regressed patients who are in need of constant supervision and care remains. Since the total number of patients is diminished, the increased economic possibilities should be directed toward improving the style of living of these fewer remaining patients. To deny the problem and to order the closing of these institutions before providing satisfactory alternatives seems unrealistic.

Some private hospitals accept some very regressed patients, but the cost is so high that only a few people can afford it. Moreover, the number of private hospitals that are willing to take care of these patients is rapidly diminishing. Every citizen should urge the legislators to do much more to implement marked improvements in the conditions of hospitals for the chronically ill mental patient.

Reintegration in the Community

If reintegration in the community is a wonderful event for the person who recovers from schizophrenia or for the patient who remains moderately ill, it is an event of rare occurrence for people who belong to the hard core that we have described in this section. We must remember that, contrary to what some authors want us to believe, the most cogent problem of these patients is not institutionalization but the seriousness of their mental condition.

In a well-intentioned but rather unrealistic move, many patients have been discharged from hospitals who have no chance of making an adjustment in a regular community. I am not against discharging patients even if they have only a small chance to make it in the outside world. I am also not disturbed by the possibility of readmitting patients and following what has been called the *revolving-door policy.* The revolving door is better than the closed door. I am of course in favor of helping these people in every possible way to go through the different stages of rehabilitation. However, there is a set of problems relating to the very sick mental patient that has to be considered. The criterion of whether the patient is dangerous to others is not the only one to be considered. The problem is how to help the patient live in a satisfactory (or less unsatisfactory) way. Many live in boarding homes that are unlicensed and poorly supervised. These patients now walk aimlessly in the streets and often sleep in the doorways of churches, railroad stations, or parts of the streets that seem less exposed to inclement weather. They often carry their bundles of hoarded objects and become unshaven, dirty, emaciated. Some of them are beaten and robbed by juvenile gangs or by drug addicts. Many communities are exasperated at the sight of these human beings and show no compassion, only resentment. If Albert Deutsch were alive, he would have good cause to write another book about the second shame of the states.

Respect of Civil Rights

The civil rights of even the very seriously mentally ill person must be respected. Commitment to an institution, even the most liberal, implies a deprivation of freedom that should not be undertaken without due process of law. Recently the criteria for committment have been markedly altered by state legislations. Involuntary hospitalization is generally applicable when the patient's imminent danger to himself or others can be demonstrated. Remote or distant possibility of harm to oneself or others is in most states no longer sufficient.

Since 1960 the right-to-treatment movement has gained

momentum. If an institution cannot give evidence of providing adequate treatment for each individual patient who is detained involuntarily, the patient must be released at his request. It is difficult, of course, to define the standards of adequate treatment for the mental patient who is chronically and seriously ill. For those who have reached the most advanced stages of regression, no treatment is adequate. Certainly the environment should be humane, the professional staff should be quantitatively and qualitatively adequate, and each patient should receive at least a minimum of individual consideration. But are these characteristics sufficient for the classification *adequate treatment?* Patients do have other rights that are still debated in some legal and psychiatric circles. One of them is the right to the least restrictive treatment. If a treatment that could be substituted for involuntary confinement is available, that type of treatment should be chosen.

Many believe that no matter how ill the patient is, he has the right to refuse psychosurgery, electroshock, medication, and even psychotherapy. I support the abolition of psychosurgery. The irrevocability of the damage to the brain, which precludes the application of either new methods devised in the future or additional unforeseeable opportunities, should convince anyone not to resort to this type of treatment. When I have recommended other types of treatment, I have always succeeded in convincing the patient to accept them. However, I realize that it may be difficult to do so with a few seriously ill patients who refuse to accept any kind of treatment. Even with the very few for whom, practically, there is very little or no hope of improvement with present types of treatment, it may be advisable not to exert pressure. At least the patient will retain the feeling that to some extent he still directs his life.

The question of the respect for the civil rights of patients is also being vigorously discussed in the United Kingdom. The Mental Health Act of 1957 made sweeping changes in patients' rights, but is now being reexamined as to its relevance to modern psychiatry. Many people practising within the area of mental health care have been active in these arguments, although the main thrust for reform has come from voluntary bodies, of which the most prominent in the United Kingdom is the National Association for Mental Health (MIND).

Final Remarks

What general orientation must we have toward the seriously and chronically mentally ill patient?

1. The community must be educated to acquire a more tolerant attitude toward these human beings. First of all, we must reassure the community that they are no more dangerous than an equal number of people who have never suffered from a schizophrenic disorder.

2. Legislators must be alerted to the compelling necessity of providing shelter and decent living arrangements for the mentally ill. Perhaps some old state hospitals could be modified into living quarters where people are kept with the minimum amount of regulation necessary for proper functioning.

3. We must dismantle the myth, conceived by some optimistic persons, that aftercare in the community for very regressed persons is cheaper than keeping them in institutions. If we want to provide for them in ways superior to the present inadequate ones, society must be prepared to spend more money. In any attempt to help, to save, to rescue, the guidelines must be not what is the most economical but what will come closest to our therapeutic aims.

The humane treatment of the hard core of very regressed schizophrenics is not exclusively, or even predominantly, a psychiatric problem. It is a problem that involves society as a whole. Society must intervene and take over the major responsibility. The degree of civilization achieved by a society can be revealed by what that society does for its irreparably ill. The humanitarian spirit of a people can be actualized in no better way than in a compassionate and cooperative attitude toward such patients. Conversely, the degree of savagery to which a society has descended can be demonstrated by what it plans to do for the sick. The most recent example of savagery was the 'solution' for seriously mentally ill persons that Nazi Germany put into effect during World War II.

10. Special Situations

Therapeutic Assistants and Psychiatric Companions

In former years I resorted quite frequently to the help of a therapeutic assistant or a psychiatric companion in the treatment and rehabilitation of patients who remained moderately to severely ill and continued to live with the family. The reason I fell back on this procedure much more frequently in the past than at present is due to a combination of factors.

1. It has become more difficult to find people willing to work in this capacity, especially with young male patients.

2. The rising cost of this procedure has made it less accessible to most people.

3. Drug therapy (which did not exist when this procedure was started), with consequent amelioration of symptoms, has made less necessary – although still desirable in some cases – the aid of a companion or an assistant.

4. In the intervening years established concepts about the role of the family in the patient's psychodynamics have been reevaluated.

These reasons have been incentives for enlisting the cooperation of family members in the ways described in Chapter 8, thus limiting the use of the therapeutic assistant to special situations only.

The special situations exist when the requirements of the patient are immense and cannot be met by the relatives, or when the emotional involvement of the family has become too complex, too full of conflict, and impossible to modify. In these instances the use of an outsider in the capacity of therapeutic assistant or psychiatric companion may make hospitalization unnecessary.

A psychiatrically trained nurse, a person with a great deal of empathy and understanding, or a person who has been successfully analyzed or who has undergone psychodynamic psychotherapy may become a competent therapeutic companion. Like the psychiatrist John Rosen, who introduced this procedure, I have used former psychotic patients for this purpose. The experiences that they have previously undergone add a new and rich dimension to those qualities already mentioned. Of course, not all former patients are suitable, and only a minority of them are willing to share again mental illness at its depth. When they are willing, however, the effects are usually very rewarding. The therapeutic companion is there to help, to support, to share.

At a certain stage of the treatment the assistant is particularly valuable. When the patient, as a result of psychotherapy, has lost delusions and hallucinations, he may nevertheless retain a vague feeling of being threatened – a feeling that is abstract and diffuse, and from which he tries to defend himself by withdrawing. The therapeutic companion is there to dispel that feeling. The companion is also available when a family member cannot be because of work commitments or other reasons. Somebody exists on whom the patient can rely for long stretches of time. The therapeutic assistant paves the way to the external world, removes the fear of the environment. Of course, the fear could not be overcome without the much deeper inner work done with the therapist. But the therapeutic companion is there to offer a concrete link between the psychodynamic understanding, the new relatedness with the therapist, and the external world. The assistant shows in an immediate way that the many things the patient is afraid of do not exist and have no power to hurt. In many cases the therapeutic assistant appears to the patient more convincing and more reassuring than a member of the family.

When the patient's symptoms are weakening, the work of the therapeutic companion may hasten their disappearance. For instance, the patient may not wish to go to the store for fear of persecutors or because he is fearful of making a wrong choice. In the company of the therapeutic companion, however, the patient will go; he will be able to make choices; he will see no persecutors.

In many cases the therapeutic companion may help the patient better than any family member to overcome some habits and symptoms that are harmful and disruptive and increase the patient's detachment from the rest of the world. Unless corrected, these habits perpetuate themselves and tend to become ingrained in the whole life of the patient. They are, however, not as resistant as they seem. Often the warm feeling of being together with another human being is enough to make the patient drop his habits. The therapist may not be aware of these disruptive habits, either because they do not occur during the sessions or because they are unnoticed. The family members, on the other hand, are so used to them and have learned to take them for granted that they do not even bother to mention them to the therapist. The therapeutic assistant will observe them, report them to the therapist, and correct them in a kind way.

What I have said about habits or general behavior applies also to symptoms. It may be useful here to repeat and elaborate on some procedures already mentioned in Chapter 8 in reference to family members. Many therapists do not know when a patient is going to hallucinate or act out the content of his hallucinations. But the therapeutic assistant knows, sometimes because of his familiarity with the patient's facial expression or body posture, that in a few minutes he is going to hallucinate and maybe act out the experience with impulsive behavior. The therapeutic companion gently goes to him, distracts him, and involves him in other activities so that the possibility of hallucinating is lessened. Whereas the therapist tries to interpret the symptoms and make them unnecessary, the therapeutic assistant offers the patient ways to *avert* them. This aversion therapy has nothing to do with mechanical conditioned-reflex therapy, but it has to do with the warm intervention of another human being. By aversion of symptoms, I mean creating situations in which symptoms are not likely to occur and avoiding situations in which they may easily happen. For instance, if the patient has the tendency to indulge in rituals when he is alone, he should be left alone as little as possible. Aversion therapy is much more than symptomatic treatment; symptoms and habits become stronger and more resistant the more frequently they occur.

There is a tendency on the part of some patients who are helped by a therapeutic companion to return to a condition of early childhood, to see the assistant as a mother-nurse. But even better than family members, the therapeutic assistant is able to nourish without stultifying the growth of the patient and to exert a push that is not harsh and therefore resented, but kind and soft. The feeling of · intense relatedness for the patient – rather than preconceived ideas, planned programs, or daily activities – will indicate to the therapeutic assistant when to practice the gentle push to combat a tendency to be inactive or to withdraw.

Several complications may develop in the work of the therapeutic assistant. Many of them involve the assistant as a person, such as undergoing feelings of countertransference similar to those of the therapist. In quite a few cases the therapeutic companion tends to see the patient as a person who needs help very much, even when he has improved considerably. The companion may be unwilling to spend less time with the patient, or to decrease care. He may have developed such strong feelings of affection for the patient that it may be difficult to stop working with him. And yet this counter-transference was a necessity for a good therapeutic relationship. All these feelings have to be analyzed and a solution for them found in the periodic meetings that the therapist and the therapeutic assistant must have.

Another difficulty lies in the hostility that the patient in some cases develops for the companion, either because he resents being dependent, because he is afraid of the warmth he has for the assistant, or because he identifies him with an important figure in his past and sees him through paranoid distortions. All these situations, of course, must be reported to the therapist, who will discuss them with the patient.

So-called triangular situations may develop in which therapist and therapeutic companion compete or seem to work against each other because of the manipulations of the patient. If the patient feels that there is disagreement between the therapist and the therapeutic companion about his own treatment or between the therapist or therapeutic companion and a parent, he is bound to become disturbed. The disturbance in some cases is caused by a reactivation of the feeling the patient used to have in his childhood, that he was the cause or the victim of the dissension that existed between his parents. When the problems are openly discussed with the patient and the misunderstanding or different emphasis clarified, the disturbance quickly disappears.*

Emergencies

In comparison to other branches of medicine, there are few serious emergencies in psychiatry. There are no conditions comparable to a ruptured appendix, a perforated ulcer, a strangulated hernia, or a coronary attack in psychiatry. Most psychiatric patients, even if suffering from serious psychiatric disorders, can wait at least twenty-four hours before seeing a psychiatrist. However, a few emergencies do occur in psychiatry, too. Thus it is imperative that the family members communicate the emergency to a doctor. If no doctor is available, they should take the patient to a hospital. Many general hospitals have an emergency psychiatric clinic or a walk-in clinic, where a psychiatrist examines the patient right away, gives him first aid, and makes the necessary recommendations.

If the hospital is reached by phone, the family members must ask whether that hospital is provided with a psychiatric acute care service. In some localities these emergency units are easy to find. For instance, in New York County (Borough of Manhattan) there are nine hospitals provided with such service. The family member must be ready to provide the address of the patient to determine whether he belongs to the 'catchment area' or section of the city covered by that particular hospital. In the large cities of the United Kingdom most of the general hospitals provide a twenty-four-hour emergency cover service for psychiatric cases.

In some geographical areas it may be difficult to find acute care units. However, the information office of any hospital will be able to indicate the name of the nearest hospital provided with that service.

Fortunately the number of schizophrenics who need such services is not as large as one would think – not as large as that of

* See also Sally Lorraine, 'The Therapeutic Assistant in Treating the Psychotic,' *International Journal of Psychiatry*, Vol. 10 (1972): 11-22.

drug addicts, acute manics, alcoholics, or seriously depressed patients who threaten suicide. However, a state of emergency may develop also for the schizophrenic patient. He, too, may be suicidal, homicidal, assaultive, querulous, noisy to an unbearable degree, or given to uncontrollable antisocial impulses. Because of their conspicuousness, such patients seem numerous, but actually, in comparison to the total number of schizophrenics, they are not. In Amsterdam, a city of almost a million people, municipal medical and health services have a world-famous service for psychiatric emergencies. The service is said to receive so few calls that after midnight the psychiatrist on duty goes to bed and is seldom disturbed. At least until a few years ago, at such twenty-four-hour walk-in clinics as those of the Massachusetts Mental Health Center in Boston and the Malcolm Bliss Mental Health Center in St Louis, few persons required care after midnight.

Some authors have defined *emergency* as any case that has to be seen right away and cannot be handled by facilities existing in the community. Others (H. Resnik and H. Ruben) have defined an emergency as ' a sudden, unforeseen, isolated incident which, if unresponded to, will result in life-threatening or psychologically damaging consequences.'

In an emergency service most cases that do not involve schizophrenics concern marital problems, parent-child fights, traumatic sexual experiences, sudden death of a close relative or friend, and consequences of intoxication, alcoholism, or drugs. In most of these cases it is relatively easy to determine the precipitating or stressful events. Some authors (L. Bellak and L. Small) have described a form of emergency psychotherapy that is applied in special situations of crisis. It ranges from one to six therapeutic sessions and requires a very active role on the part of the therapist. This emergency therapy is not indicated for schizophrenic patients.

With schizophrenic patients the matter is more complicated. Some of them unexpectedly become dangerous to themselves and make suicidal attempts in answer to commands from hallucinatory voices. Others become dangerous to others, again because of aggressive orders received from the voices. Not rare are paranoid patients who disclose aggressive tendencies toward imaginary persecutors from whom they intend to defend themselves. A situation of emergency becomes obvious when the patient shows assaultive, aggressive, or destructive behavior. Other patients are considered in a state of emergency when they display agitated confusion, disorientation, excitement, and grossly bizarre and antisocial behavior. Schizophrenics who arouse great anxiety among relatives and people at large and bring about emergency intervention tend to act on their delusions, not in a suicidal or homicidal way, but with unacceptable, bizarre behavior. People tolerate patients who write distressing letters and even destroy property, but not those who masturbate, defecate, or urinate in public, or who are exhibitionistic or child-molesters. It is important to stress that *it has never been demonstrated that these categories exist in larger numbers among schizophrenics than among nonschizophrenics.*

Assaultive paranoid patients are a very small minority but may cause much trouble because they are very difficult to handle and can become dangerous. A patient generally becomes dangerous when he is afraid. Even patients who seem docile may change when faced with treatment that appears threatening to them and reinforces their delusional thinking. This brings up the question of whether the police should be called when an emergency arises or assault on the part of the paranoid patient seems likely.

The intervention of the police is unavoidable in a certain percentage of cases. Unfortunately there are no other provisions or groups equipped to handle these cases. In many localities even the prompt request for an ambulance has to be made through the police. Disturbing thoughts come to mind in connection with obtaining help from the police. First of all, police deal with violators of law, and therefore it is repugnant to us to have sick people treated by policemen. Moreover, many paranoid patients will be reinforced in their delusions of being persecuted and victimized by organized society. On the other hand, in addition to the fact that in some cases no other means are available, many policemen have developed a degree of sophistication in dealing with mentally disturbed people of which professionals are envious.

Somehow they know how to reassure the patient or to make him control his aggressive behavior.

A minority of cases of psychiatric emergencies cannot be brought to hospitals or to other psychiatric facilities. In these rare occasions it is a professional who must go to visit the patient at home. Many psychiatrists are very reluctant to make home visits, but most of them know young colleagues who have just started to practice and who have time available to make such visits. The most common reason for a psychiatric home visit is making a diagnosis and determining whether the patient requires hospitalization or not. A psychiatrist may also call at the patient's home if a severe physical disability such as coronary attack, crippling arthritis, or stroke is present. The third important occasion for a home visit is the refusal of the patient to go out of the house, either because of paranoid fears or other delusions, or because, in addition to schizophrenic symptoms, the patient has phobias that prevent him from leaving his home.

Whenever possible, the patient should be induced to go to a psychiatric facility, even for an emergency. The feeling that he has the power to make the psychiatrist come to his home may persuade the patient that he can control the therapeutic situation, and this feeling may delay improvement.

The Joining of Esoteric Cults

A considerable number of parents of former schizophrenic patients or patients who have recovered only to a moderate degree or have become chronically ill often consult a psychiatrist because their child has joined an esoteric cult. They do not see him any more. In other cases the particular cult they have joined permits them to remain at home, but they seem interested only in the practice of the cult and in talking about the mythology of the cult. What can the parents do? This situation, although much more common today, is not completely new. It has its roots in similar events that occurred before the flourishing of new cults.

Since the beginning of my psychiatric practice I have seen a certain number of preschizophrenics, schizophrenics, and partially recovered schizophrenics convert to a new religion. They have thus fulfilled several goals: (1) they rebelled against their parents; (2) they tried to find in the new religion a solution to their problems, which they thought could not be solved if things remain unchanged; and (3) they tried desperately to make some satisfactory inter-personal relationships, though in a very unusual form (convent, missionary work, mystical group, and so forth). Generally, the change in religion was from one to another of the major religions of the Western countries. Today the situation has changed. First of all, in addition to the goals listed above, there is a more pronounced dissatisfaction with society. This dissatisfaction is not manifested in political ways as it was in the students' confrontations of the 1960s, but in the adoption of new mystical views of the world. Although a few cults continue to be based on modifications of Judeo-Christian ideology or on specific political orientations, the majority of them are based on Hindu and Eastern concepts. Some of them are involved with witchcraft and strange forms of spiritualism.

Lest I be misunderstood, I wish to clarify a point. By no means do I state or imply that all or most of the people who join these groups are schizophrenics, mentally ill, or maladjusted. I do not know of any statistical work that has demonstrated this. Moreover, I know that ideological movements, even those that later proved to have been beneficial to humanity, in the beginning attracted a large number of people who were not only discontented but more or less mentally disturbed. What I am in a position to say is only that a statistically significant number of people, with whom I have come into contact for professional reasons and whose difficulties were in a gray area between mental illness and social maladjustment, did join cults. In addition to them, a considerable number of people who could be classified as preschizophrenics, former schizophrenics, partially recovered schizophrenics, or chronic schizophrenics also joined these groups. Practically all these people belonged to middle-class, upper middle-class, and upper-class families.

Psychologist Margaret T. Singer has written an excellent paper, 'Therapy with Ex-Cult Members.' Her article is rather optimistic. She writes that ' these individuals have much anger toward the cult for having used and controlled them. They have anger and concern over lost years and opportunities. They have a fear of the future and anxieties about what will happen if they don't get their lives going at the level that they would like.'

To neutralize the conditioning and indoctrination of the cult, Singer offers a great deal of information, support, and assistance. According to her, 'deprogramming' is not an atrocity, as it has been described by the cults to the press, but 'nothing more than an intense period of information giving.' Although I am not absolutely sure, I believe that Dr Margaret Singer has dealt with people less sick than those who have come to my attention and predominantly not schizophrenics.

Dr Singer describes very well what these cults offer: 'simplistic answers' to the problems of life. They 'supply their members with ready-made friends and ready-made decisions about careers, dating, sex and marriage, and the 'meaning of life.' In return, they demand total obedience, which they maintain through various programs of coercive persuasion.' Some cult organizations have indoctrinated their members to go out on the street and raise money. They cannot come back until they have raised $150 or more, even if this implies working steadily from eighteen to twenty-four hours.

To Dr Singer's accurate remarks I wish to add that one of the apparent advantages of the cult is that it eliminates or decreases the importance of the dyadic relationship. This also occurs in some communes. A dyadic relationship is that existing between two persons (husband and wife, parent and child); it requires a degree of intimacy, commitment, and interchange that no other inter-personal relationship does. By becoming a part of a cult, a person substitutes the group and the psychologically simpler group relationship for the dyadic one.

How do I feel about these cults? I want again to stress that my answer refers only to the schizophrenic group (which includes pre-schizophrenics, former schizophrenics, moderately ill schizo-phrenics, and chronic schizophrenics) and not to all the people included in Dr Singer's study. My feeling is that it is indeed a very sad state of affairs when a person has to surrender his own individuality, autonomy, and independence and join an esoteric group in order to maintain even a marginal mental equilibrium. Nevertheless, this is at present the case with some human beings. I believe that joining these groups has prevented some persons who could not find better ways of rehabilitation from regressing indefinitely. Moreover, some patients have found the type of life offered by the cult to be more satisfactory than that offered by current methods of rehabilitation. Apparently these persons do not focus on what they lose by joining the group (freedom, initiative, spontaneity) but on what they get (protection and freedom from making decisions and from other such demands).

When parents ask me what to do with a youngster who wants to join or has joined a cult, my answer is the following: First, if the child is over eighteen I remind the parents that legally there is nothing they can do unless they can demonstrate that the son or daughter is treated with cruelty, starvation, violence, slavery, coerced drug use, or similar practices. If the parents cannot give evidence for such conditions but strongly believe that they exist, they should inform local authorities or contact their Congressional representative and stimulate the government to take proper actions to prevent similar abuses. Second, if the patient belongs to the schizophrenic group, we have to evaluate whether what was offered to him in terms of rehabilitation is better than what the cult is offering him. Third, it may be dangerous to 'deprogram' a schizophrenic. It is indeed a great accomplishment to 'program' a schizophrenic. The deprogramming may bring about a state of complete disintegration. Programming, if actually achieved, may improve the conditions of the patient in a way similar to that of the token economy program given to very regressed schizophrenics. In my opinion, the worst aspects of programming and cult indoctrination are that they make patients belonging to the schizophrenic groups totally impervious to psychotherapy.

Perhaps when I enlarge my experience with a greater number of schizophrenics who are ex-cult members, I shall revise my statement; but at the present time I must say that I could not go very far with even one of them. The indoctrination was the barrier between me and the patient. This barrier also protected the patient from the world outside the cult group. But the barrier that protected and secluded him from a richer life also protected him from further regression.

For me, one of the most regrettable aspects of this whole issue is that it demonstrates that cults have been able to reach a large number of these disturbed people even when we, workers in the field of mental health, have not. Another unfortunate aspect of the situation is that we cannot in all conscience discourage some people (directly or through their parents) from joining these groups when our present methods of rehabilitating the chronically ill have so few and such inadequate facilities, with the result that a considerable number of these persons wander aimlessly in the streets, in the ways described on page 180 of this book. If society were more responsive to the plight of these people, cult organizations would be less popular. Perhaps we should not condemn these organizations *a priori* but study them with great humility, so that we can absorb what is useful in them and applicable to other communities. If we can do that and at the same time eliminate whatever in these cult groups is undesirable (such as limitation of individuality and free choice), we may be able to achieve results that so far have eluded us.

Addendum

A few days after the manuscript of this book was delivered to the publisher the unhappy news was received of the massacre that occurred in Jonestown, Guyana, of the followers of the People's Temple, founded by James Jones. Although we should never make the mistake of putting all cults into one category, the necessity of further investigation and of distinguishing one group from the other seems more urgent after this tragedy that resulted in the deaths of more than 900 persons. Because cults at first seem to offer acceptance and easy solutions to complex problems, they attract persons who feel rejected or overwhelmed by the difficulties of life. Among them are many who belong to the schizophrenic group, as described above. However, later on in some cults mystical rituals, indoctrination, infatuation with charismatic leaders, lack of privacy, sleep deprivation, and poor nutrition make it extremely difficult for individual members to liberate themselves from the yoke imposed by the collective system. Again my strong wish is that society will offer other solutions to fellow citizens who are in desperate psychological need.

11. Prevention

To anyone who is concerned with schizophrenia, nothing can be more important than its prevention. In the field of psychiatry, preventive medicine has made tremendous progress in at least three areas: (1) psychosis due to pellagra, (2) general paresis, and (3) delirium due to infective conditions.

These three conditions were recognized as being brought about exclusively by physical causes. It was enough to prevent pellagra with a diet rich in vitamins, general paresis with timely antisyphilitic treatment, and delirium with administration of sulfonamides and antibiotics.

As we saw in Chapter 5, the causes of schizophrenia are more complicated and completely different from those of the three conditions above. Because of its many complex ramifications, the prevention of schizophrenia has not up to now received the attention that it deserves. Recently, however, throughout the United States psychiatrists and psychologists have become much more concerned with the prevention of mental disease in general. Centers for genetic counseling, family therapy, and low-cost individual and group counseling are being opened in many cities and towns. Although our efforts in the field of the prevention of schizophrenia are still at a pioneer stage, they are already appreciated and worthy of full consideration. This book has demonstrated that in spite of the questionable points about the cause of schizophrenia, the knowledge that we possess is extensive and definite enough to enable us to implement measures likely to exert effective preventive action.

Three types of prevention will be discussed. They are as follows:

1. *Basic prevention*, which aims at the elimination of those prerequisites, either hereditary or environmental, that create a potentiality for schizophrenia or increase vulnerability to it.

2. *Longitudinal prevention*, which aims at assisting the individual throughout his life – especially his early life – to avoid those circumstances, developments, or lasting situations that will enhance the risk of transforming what was only a potential for or predisposition to the actual clinical appearance of schizophrenia.

3. *Critical prevention*, which attempts to help the potential schizophrenic avoid specific stressful events that can cause schizophrenia to occur.

Basic Prevention

Heredity

We have seen in Chapter 5 that there is almost certain evidence that a potential for schizophrenia has a hereditary basis. Let us clearly restate, however, that, according to the present state of our knowledge, schizophrenia is not inherited – only a vulnerability or potential for it is. A definite prevention thus would consist of making impossible the transmission of such hereditary predisposition from generation to generation, so that even if individuals were exposed to the most stressful and trying psychological experiences, they would not develop the illness. However, it is unfeasible, as well as undesirable, to put into effect these preventive measures. Schizophrenia puts us in a situation quite different from that with which we are confronted in relationship to well-known hereditary diseases. In a family where Huntington's chorea, muscular dystrophy, hemophilia, and other unquestionably hereditary conditions exist, the physician can easily explain to the individual the Mendelian laws of inheritance, the existence of genes that are either dominant or recessive, and the possible risk for children. In the case of schizophrenia, similarly clear genetic counseling is impossible. The counselor can only say that if a parent is a schizophrenic, the risk of the child's developing schizophrenia is increased in comparison to that of the general population, but that he still has at least a 90 to 95 percent probability of *not* developing schizophrenia.

If it is not feasible to prevent marriages of people who are carriers of definite hereditary diseases, it is much more difficult to do so in the cases of schizophrenia, when the literature on the subject seems to guarantee at least 90 percent protection. In other words, if a person is or has been a schizophrenic, he has a 10 percent chance of transmitting schizophrenia by heredity. If an individual had a parent who was a schizophrenic, he also has a 10 percent chance of becoming a schizophrenic. *The probability exists that if other preventive psychological measures are followed, the 10 percent potential will never become a reality.* The fact that the statistics are not so overwhelming, and the possibility that environmental factors may neutralize them completely, induce people to follow love and moral considerations rather than the genetic risk. Moreover, the individual may be strengthened in his or her determination to provide a good environment and may undergo preventive psychotherapy. Lifetime birth control, voluntary sterilization, or therapeutic abortion cannot be authoritatively recommended in the presence of such relatively little risk. Such measures should be recommended, however, when both spouses are or have been schizophrenics, because statistics indicate that in these cases the risk of schizophrenia in the children is very high (from 50 to 68 percent). The following conclusions can be drawn:

1. It is difficult (and perhaps not justified) to counsel against marriage, or at least against parenthood, people who are possibly carriers of a hereditary predisposition to schizophrenia unless a considerable or great risk exists. The risk is great in the case of two prospective parents who both suffered or are suffering from the illness.

2. When a hereditary predisposition for schizophrenia exists, and patients and their fiancés want to proceed with their marital plans, counseling should be given in order to establish a favorable family environment and decrease the risk of the illness.

Early Environment

At the present stage of our knowledge it seems almost certain that a hereditary predisposition to schizophrenia can be counteracted by a healthy early environment. Thus the prevention of schizophrenia should be oriented toward the elimination of those circumstances that are likely to bring about a psychologically unhealthy environment.

Parents' Marriage. The unhappy marriage of the parents is one of the fundamental and most common determinants of an unhealthy early environment. Whatever is negative in the personality of each parent tends to become accentuated in an unhappy marital situation. It is true that there are many unhappy marriages and that in only a small percentage of them do we find schizophrenic children. Not only must the hereditary predisposition be there, and many other circumstances, but the unhappy marriage must also be unfavorable to the children to such an extent as to prevent them from identifying satisfactorily with either parent or obtaining a modicum of security.

A survey of families of schizophrenic patients reveals that marital unhappiness is more common and more pronounced than in the families of the general population. There are apparent exceptions. At times the illness of the patient brings about a feeling of solidarity between the parents and reinforces their bond. These are usually late events and, unless investigated and corrected by professional counseling, in some cases may be more harmful to the patient than helpful. A marriage that requires the patient to be ill in order to maintain itself does not have a genuine or worthwhile foundation. Prospective mates who know beforehand that from a hereditary point of view they will give birth to high-risk children should be counseled and become familiar with the involvements and commitments of married life.

Parenthood. Unhappily married people may find psychological satisfaction and compensation in raising children, especially in some cultures where parenthood is considered the most important aspect of marriage. In these circumstances children are not seriously impaired. On the other hand, in a culture where the significance or importance of parenthood is diminished or is secondary to the other aspects of marriage, unhappily married people tend also to be poor parents. From the time of the Industrial Revolution to the present, and especially since technological changes have occurred at a very rapid pace, our culture and society have been in a state of transition. There have been changes in the roles of mother and father that constitute threats to traditional parenthood. When these cultural factors are reinforced by personality difficulties, the consequences may be undesirable.

Modern woman is reevaluating many traditional values and functions. At the same time she recognizes (even if until very recently she has not openly expressed) her resentment of the fact that in a predominantly patriarchal society she has often been considered a second-class citizen and has not been given opportunities equal to those given to men. In her efforts to achieve equality she now diverts some of her energy from the function of housewife and seeks a career as a man does. She is certainly entitled and justified. But just as society failed her before for putting her in a state of submission, it fails her now for not preparing her adequately for a double role. The task is indeed difficult, and sociologists should study the problem more adequately, not just along theoretical lines but along practical ones. Married women must have a feeling of fulfillment, otherwise they will experience frustration and may need to compete with their husbands, with resulting family unhappiness.

One function that a woman cannot change is motherhood. But for this function she should not be required to give up many other important aspects of life. A considerable number of mothers have difficulties in the urban-industrial society. In this environment many young women have not been sufficiently prepared for motherhood. Some of them see no beauty or challenge in being mothers. Obviously these women should not be criticized or abandoned but helped to reevaluate their perception of motherhood while maintaining the possibility of a career. In our modern Western society, which aims at equality of the two sexes, the role of the father should also be redefined, and many of the functions originally assigned exclusively to women should be more fairly distributed.

Focusing on a career and competing with men are not the only reasons that make preparation for motherhood more difficult. Natalie Shainess, in illustrating the psychological problems associated with motherhood, has reminded us of Freud's stress on the woman's double sexual role and its consequences: first, attracting and having a sexual relationship with a man; second, giving birth to children and assuming the mothering task. Some mothers are successful only in the first role; many mothers, however, are not successful in either. They enter marriage expecting a great deal and are not prepared to give in return. After the arrival of the child, some of these mothers experience motherhood as a stress.

Society should help young women to reacquire a sense of purpose in motherhood. It would be advisable for young girls in high school and college to receive some counseling and education. In this transitional time, when the role of women is being redefined, many of them have not learned adequately about motherhood through a process of identification with their own mothers. Courses, theoretical instructions, and even counseling offered in a scholastic setting may appear as too scientific, artificial, and premeditated methods of instilling love for motherhood. They very easily can be. The present state of affairs, however, is that a certain percentage of women, because of social changes, have lost that spontaneous, natural attitude toward motherhood that used to be transmitted from generation to generation. Until women have recognized this socially induced situation, we must resort to any method that can help them.

Fatherhood, too, has become less satisfactory since the time of the Industrial Revolution. Mitscherlich and Mitscherlich have described 'the invisible father' in our society. The father is no longer the teacher, the senior partner in artisanry. He has lost authority not only as a teacher of life but also as an enforcer of discipline, as a giver of examples to imitate, as a person with whom children can identify. Often he is relegated to the role of a playmate. He sees the children seldom, and when he does see them he wants to be one of them, to play with them, to be their peer. But in doing so, he soon loses his parental status. Obviously in the state of change present society is in, fatherhood has to undergo a transformation. Not all the changes described by the Mitscherlichs are necessarily negative. However, modern fathers have not yet defined their new role, and this state of indecision may lead to conflict and family instability. Like modern mothers, modern fathers, too, need help. Help should also be provided for future fathers similar to that suggested for future mothers.

In summary, at the present state of our knowledge it seems probable that an adverse early psychological environment can be avoided by all those sociological and psychological measures that prevent unhappy marriages and promote good motherhood and fatherhood.

Longitudinal Prevention

Longitudinal prevention aims at modifying the effects of an adverse early environment, and at affecting social conditions in such a way that essential needs are more easily fulfilled for the child, adolescent, and young adult and that unusual stress does not exceed the capacity of the individual to cope with it.

Longitudinal prevention is often difficult because the family is reluctant to seek professional intervention before the need is very obvious, and also because society at large (and a certain sector of medical and scholastic authorities) is insensitive to psychological problems.

Personally, I believe that a psychiatric or psychological examination should be required for every student, at least in grammar school and high school, and that parents should be informed of the results. If the examiner discovers the first signs of personal abnormalities, he may suggest individual psychotherapy for the student; recommend counseling, family therapy, or therapy for the parents; or suggest changes in the environment of the child, adolescent, young adult, or adult. In some cases it is useful to enlarge the family circle. In the traditional family the child was exposed to many influences: not only to parents and one or two siblings but also to several brothers and sisters, grandparents, uncles, aunts, cousins, and various other persons. Today families, especially in large cities, consist of the parents and one or two children. Thus there is no possibility of compensation for the children or of identification with other individuals if the parents, for whatever reason, cannot offer good parenthood.

In many cases the examiner can recommend that the child or adolescent be under the influence of additional adults, not just the parents. An aunt, an uncle, or a good friend of the family may steer the youngster toward a good psychological integration. A more specific suggestion is the sharing of mothering with a nonrelative. Experience in the *kibbutzim* of Israel suggests that it may be helpful for the child to have the role of mothering divided among several adults. In the *kibbutzim*, a person called a *metapelet* has the job of caring for children, of fulfilling the role of motherhood while the mother is absent. She is, essentially, a substitute mother to the children of the community. Bruno Bettelheim,* a well-known psychologist, studied children who grew up in *kibbutzim* and reported that among them he found no cases of schizophrenia. Bettelheim notes that the security needs of a child raised in a *kibbutz* originate not only from his mother and father, but also from the *metapelets* and the community in which they live. Thus, we may conclude that nonparental influences can be very helpful for the vulnerable child and are to be strongly recommended if intervention is needed. Removal from home is not necessary if these additional influences are provided.

In some instances, however, removal from the family may become necessary. This occurs when the danger is clear-cut and unavoidable. Some carefully selected boarding schools may be quite helpful in these situations.

Social conditions not related to family life have been linked to an increased rate of schizophrenia. In fact, any factor that contributes to stress can be said to be harmful to vulnerable individuals. However, research has focused on a few specific factors. Immigrants to the United States have been found to have a higher rate of schizophrenia than natives. Unmarried people have a higher rate of schizophrenia than married people. Big-city dwellers have a higher rate of schizophrenia than people living in small towns. It is very difficult to alter these circumstances. On the other hand, there are

* B. Bettelheim, *The Children of the Dream* (New York: Macmillan, 1967).

social conditions that can be prevented, such as poverty, inadequate housing, crime, prejudice, and drug addiction. The elimination of these conditions will be a wonderful thing, not only in itself, but also because it will indirectly decrease those conditions of stress that facilitate the occurrence of schizophrenia.

Critical Prevention

Critical prevention consists of helping the patient in the presence of crises that are likely to precipitate a schizophrenic episode. The first question is whether it is feasible to attempt this type of prevention. One may think that the critical and possibly precipitating event may be only the straw that broke the camel's back and that we cannot go through life avoiding or compensating for all possible straws. We have seen in Chapter 2 that this is not the case. It is not true – even when the ground for the illness has been prepared by hereditary factors, early environment, and long-standing psychological patterns – that any stressful event is a precipitating event. It must be one that is intimately or symbolically related to the total psychological picture of the patient, one that will affect his special vulnerability and deeply injure his self-image, like the traffic accident in the case of the veteran reported in Chapter 2.

Unfortunately, in many cases it is impossible to know in advance the meaning that a particular event may have for a certain person and the possible consequences. Thus critical prevention may be extremely difficult. In many other cases we know that a certain situation will present a real challenge to the patient. We also know that whereas a difficult situation or even a crisis may mobilize a normal person's resources and have a maturing effect, it may have disintegrating effects on a vulnerable person. And yet we are not in a position to make the patient avoid that situation. To restrict the patient's actions would mean to control the constitutional rights of the individual. To prevent him from taking certain steps would be tantamount to inflicting demoralization that may also precipitate the breakdown. Among such events are going away from home to college or to work; becoming engaged or married; having a baby; changing school or job; going on an adventurous trip; being promoted; ending an engagement, a marriage, or a long relationship;

and so forth. Psychiatric experience confirms that these events may indeed cause an imbalance between the demands of the new challenge and the psychological resources of the individual. It is true that, had the ground not been prepared by hereditary and previous psychological factors, the new challenge would not have produced the imbalance. Nevertheless, we cannot deny the effect of the challenge itself.

In rare cases the challenge may be brought about by what is generally considered a good event, like a promotion. The patient is now afraid that he will not be able to cope with the additional requirements caused by his new position. Failing after having obtained success is harder to bear. In order to prevent life crises we must offer interpersonal intervention that will make it easier to cope with the new situation, and we must alleviate the hazardous circumstances.

Examples of the first requirements were given in Chapter 2, when we discussed students in college who are away from the protective environment of the home for the first time. Alleviation of hazards is something difficult or impossible to put into practice without infringing upon the rights of the patient. We should not hide from him our appraisal of the situation. But if he persists in wanting to go ahead with his plans, rather than antagonizing him, we must help him to diminish the risks involved in what he wants to do. It may be simply a trip abroad, or such a complicated thing as an engagement to an unreliable person.

If a relative is not able to help the individual during a crisis or an unusual challenge, professional intervention is advisable. At times brief therapy is enough to solve a crisis that otherwise may unchain a serious disturbance.

Pregnancy and childbirth can be dramatic challenges in the life of a woman. A woman who has just given birth may have to face some aspects of life that she could not foresee or that now appear undesirable to her. Usually a new mother must reevaluate herself and the way she appears to others. A woman who has emphasized her feminine charms in the past may face a major setback as she is forced to reevaluate her femininity. Her personal attractiveness, which has been such a successful aspect of her interpersonal relationships, will not have any bearing upon her new caretaking responsibilities. A woman who is doubtful of her ability to be a mother may become overwhelmed with the fear that she cannot satisfactorily take care of the baby, that motherhood is too much to cope with. Frequently the young mother herself had an inadequate upbringing at the hands of her own mother. Thus, she fears that she will do to her child what her own mother once did to her.

A severe marital conflict may become worse after the birth of a child. Because of this birth, the woman may feel stuck with her husband, with no possibility of liberation, and may blame it on the birth of the child.

The last conflict to be discussed concerns the relationship of the mother to her baby. The baby is seen as an intruder who prevents the mother from doing as she pleases, from living an independent life. She may be jealous of the love her husband gives the child, love that she feels should be given to her.

Whereas women are generally capable of overcoming conflicts or of coping with them, a few women with psychological vulnerability may not be able to master these situations. The different types of conflict that we have mentioned at times reach unpredictable proportions and cause a great deal of anxiety to the patient who has given birth or is about to give birth. She finds herself in a predicament from which she sees no escape. Inasmuch as these conflicts often remain totally or largely unconscious, they can do a large amount of damage before the clinical picture emerges. Whenever there is suspicion of conflicts that cannot be solved by the patient, or at the earliest manifestation of psychological malaise, the woman who is pregnant or has just given birth should be examined and treated by professionals. With these preventive measures many cases of postpartum schizophrenia will be avoided.

12. What Can We Learn
From Schizophrenia

Can we really learn from schizophrenia, a serious illness of the mind? Yes, we can learn a great deal. This affirmative answer does not refer to what we can learn about the illness itself, knowledge of which is predominantly a medical or a psychiatric concern. But we can learn from it about human life in general and the human predicament.

As I have expressed elsewhere, no other state of abnormality, no other illness permits us to delve so deeply into what is specific to human nature. Knowledge of schizophrenia opens to our eyes and to our understanding a panorama of the human condition that includes the cardinal problems of truth and illusion, bizarreness and creativity, grandiosity and self-abnegation, loneliness and capacity for communion, lasting suspiciousness and absolute faith, immobility and freedom of action, capacity for projection and self-accusation, surrender to love and hate, and indifference to these feelings. The schizophrenic panorama confronts us with the possibility of experiencing and understanding life with a scientific methodology, with psychological sensitivity, as well as with a frame of mind that almost seems to unite reality and unreality in a surrealistic vision.

In spite of its fascinating mysteries and yet untapped potentialities, the world of schizophrenia is certainly not to be recommended to the individual as a place where one can escape from the human predicament, or as a method with which to achieve truth and wisdom or to enhance one's spiritual aims. This statement is a truism and would not be expressed here except for the fact that it has recently been challenged by some people who idealize the schizophrenic in a romantic way, just as the tubercular patient was idealized in some novels and operas of the nineteenth century. I believe such romanticization is not useful to anybody, and least of all to the patient who has to become part of the human community again. In this chapter, however, we shall take into consideration three issues that to some extent may be made clearer by our knowledge and understanding of schizophrenia.

The Patient's Message

The Finnish psychiatrist Siirala sees the schizophrenic as a victim and as a prophet to whom nobody listens. He sees the therapist as a person who has the duty to reveal to society the prophecies of his patients. These prophecies would consist of insights into our collective sickness, into the evil deeds that we, as members of society, have committed for many generations and that we have buried so that they will not be noticed. Siirala feels that schizophrenia emerges out of a common sort of sickness, a sickness shared by so-called healthy persons. In other words, according to Siirala, schizophrenia is, at least in its origins, a social sickness.

Why has Siirala called the schizophrenic a prophet? I am not sure, but it seems to me that perhaps we can find some similarities (certainly not identity) between many schizophrenics and the prophets of the Old Testament. The Biblical prophets were extremely sensitive to evil or to surrounding hostility. They were also extremely sensitive to society's callousness about evil. Many paranoid schizophrenics behave and think as if they had a psychological radar that enables them to detect and register the world's hostility to a much greater degree than the average person. They do not want to deny evil any more. They want to unmask others who do.

Must we assess these characteristics as positive values or as manifestations of illness? To discuss whether the paranoid is delusional or a prophet is like discussing whether a dream represents irrationality or the ' real reality.' The dream is true as an experience and, as we have learned from Freud, may indeed reveal a message not easily heard when we are awake, but it transmits the truth in a distorted way. Although hostility exists in the world, the paranoid's version of it is abnormal and very much distorted. Although hostility enters into the complex and remote causation of schizophrenia, many other factors enable it to become an active part of the causation. Although hostility is an important psychological factor, many other psychological factors are involved.

The point I am trying to make is that it is true that the patient responds abnormally to the world or misinterprets the world. Nevertheless, we should not see only the negative part of this position. If we try to understand him deeply we can become aware that normality (or what we call normality) may require mental mechanisms and attitudes that are not so healthy. At times what is demanded of us is callousness, or at best indifference, to harmful and injurious stimuli. We protect ourselves by denying them, hiding them, becoming insensitive, or finding a thousand ways of rationalizing them or adjusting to them. We become a silent majority. By being so vulnerable and so sensitive, the patient may teach us to counteract our callousness. By spending so much energy in adapting, we survive and live to the best of our ability, but we pay a big price that may result in the impoverishment of a part of our personality. We may become prisoners of a more and more stringent conformism.

When the paranoid schizophrenic experiences society as a Darwinian jungle, we must remind ourselves that not the patient but Darwin himself made the first analogy in reverse order. After having studied society in Malthus's writings, Darwin, in the Galapagos Islands, saw the jungle as a reproduction of society. Inequality, competition, struggle, and power prevail in the two situations. Unless checked by human determination, power wins out in both society and jungle. The future schizophrenic or the schizophrenic is certainly not the fittest in any jungle. When he becomes ill, he is not literally a prophet but a reminder of the powers that win most of the time and say, 'Woe to the vanquished.' His is a significant voice, and yet, in spite of its significance, most of the time his voice is too humble, too weak, too deprived of adaptational value to be heard. Anyone who cares for the patient must try to hear this voice. At the same time he must help the patient escape the illness's symptoms, which deform the message. The philosopher, the dissenter, and the revolutionary lack adaptability, as does the schizophrenic, but they compensate with their evident creativity. With a few outstanding exceptions, the schizophrenic does not utilize creative tendencies as they do. If we want to hear his genuine voice and transmit his message to the world, we must overcome the obstacles built by his illness.

What is the real voice, the value that the schizophrenic tries to express before his message is distorted by the disorder? It is the basic value of the human being. The schizophrenic wants to be the sovereign of his will. He wants to be totally himself, but he does not succeed. He finds sovereigns all over, but not in himself. He attributes hostile intents to them, and he himself harbors a great deal of hostility.

Whether we are his therapist, friend, or relative, we must be willing to accept and transmit his message. This message may possibly help future generations or youngsters who are still in the process of growing. We must also try to help the patient himself. We will be in a position to help him and to transmit to him our own message if he experiences us as peers, as human beings who share his values. When he feels that some of the real or fantastic forces that disturb him disturb us, too, he will start to relate to us without distrust. By accepting his perception of hostility from a general point of view, we shall be in a position later to cut through or dismantle the delusional distortions of this hostility. Gradually the patient's main goal becomes not fighting evil but searching for love and fulfillment.

One of the points that we want to clarify in this chapter is that by helping the schizophrenic we may also help ourselves. We become less impervious to veiled hostility, less blind to what we do not want to see, more willing to take a stand and to fight for what we disapprove of, more apt to understand a voice of dissent, even if it is expressed in an awkward or exaggerated manner. We become better able to listen to words we are generally inclined to ignore because they come from sources that seem irrational, too meek, or inappropriately humble.

Schizophrenia and Society

Although the second way in which we can benefit from the knowledge of schizophrenia is related to the first, the orientation is quite different. When we discussed the causes of schizophrenia in Chapter 5 and then the prevention of schizophrenia in Chapter 11, we came to the conclusion that there is very little we can do to prevent a hereditary predisposition from being transmitted from generation to generation. There is instead a great deal we can do to prevent those factors that directly or indirectly enter into the complex causality of this disorder. But to prevent environmental factors most of the time means to improve society and to further civilization. It means to fight those inequalities and discriminations that render many people less equipped to be good parents. It means to prevent unhappy marriages and ingrown or nuclear families. It means to promote good neighbor relationships, to increase healthy human contacts, to provide good psychological supervision in schools, to offer guidance and psychotherapy. It means that we have learned that we have one more reason, and a very important reason, to fight human suffering. Human suffering leads frequently enough to mental illness in people who are predisposed to it by biological or environmental factors. Those who see the schizophrenic symptomatology fundamentally as a protest against society may help others to see that society has so far carried out those preventive measures I have just mentioned only in a pale, inadequate, or halfhearted way.

Moreover, what we discussed in the last part of Chapter 9 concerning the nucleus of patients who at this stage of our knowledge we are not able to help and who, short of new breakthroughs, may remain seriously ill can be an incentive to assume a more humanitarian and tolerant approach toward any segment of humanity.

Schizophrenia and Creativity

In this final chapter we have stated that, unlike the schizophrenic, we so-called normal people tend to remain prisoners of conformism, and in the first chapter we stated that we tend to remain prisoners of reality. The schizophrenic is not; he is a fugitive not only from conformism but from reality, too. The schizophrenic, however, is not the only human being who escapes from reality and conformism. There are other human beings who are not satisfied with the world as they have found it. Thus they want to change this world by making it more beautiful, more predictable, more comfortable, more safe, and better understood with their works of art, science, literature, philosophy. They are the creative people. The strange thing is that these creative people, too, up to a certain point, escape from the usual ways of experiencing and interpreting the world by resorting to the same mental mechanisms of the primary process, described in Chapter 4, that the schizophrenic uses. At a certain point, however, the schizophrenic, and the creative person diverge drastically. The schizophrenic is entrapped by his own deviant ways of thinking and becomes delusional or incoherent. The creative person succeeds in harmonizing primitive and deviant mental processes with the normal ones, and the result is an act or product of creativity.

For instance, Von Domarus's principle, as explained in Chapter 4, is adopted by the schizophrenic to sustain some delusions and by the creative person to pursue his process of creativity, but only during a certain stage of this process. Like the schizophrenic, the creative person relates apparently dissimilar things. Newton, for example, saw a similarity between an apple falling to the earth and the moon. Nobody else had seen that similarity. If an average person saw a similarity of this type, he would likely disregard it. Newton instead perceived the similarity between what causes an apple to fall to the earth and what holds the moon in its orbit. What was at first only an analogy became the discovery of the force of gravity.

Similarly, the metamorphosis that occurs in schizophrenic delusions becomes a metaphor in poetic creativity. The object is temporarily identified with another because of a common trait or predicate. For instance, a woman is represented as a rose because both the flower and that particular woman have at least one attribute in common: being beautiful. At times the poet has almost that capacity for imagery that the dreamer has, or that capacity for 'orgies of identification' that the schizophrenic has. In the making of metaphors, the poet uses images that could not have been predicted. For example, the French poet Victor Hugo compares the stars in numerous and, to some persons, inconceivable ways: to diamonds, jewels, golden clouds, golden pebbles, lamps, lighted temples, flowers of eternal summer, silvery lilies, eyes of the night, vague eyes of the twilight, embers of the sky, holes in a huge ceiling, bees that fly in the sky, drops of Adam's blood, and even the colored spots on the tail of the peacock.

It is beyond the purpose of this book to illustrate how the creative person harmonizes primitive thinking with high cognitive processes and thus brings about innovations in the various fields of creativity.* It is important, however, to stress two things at this point: (1) The study of the primitive mental processes of the schizophrenic may help us understand the creative process of the creative person, and (2) the schizophrenic person has primordial sources of richness in his psyche. If he recovers sufficiently, he has the potential to use them together with normal mental mechanisms, and he, too, has the possibility of becoming an innovator.

Concluding Remarks

I hope that throughout this book it has been shown that we can learn to better understand a human being who may be very difficult to understand, and to relate to him, even when he seems willing to break all human relations. I hope that behind the masks imposed by the schizophrenic illness we have recognized a person who has feelings and aspirations similar to ours and a capacity for suffering as we do, a person who indeed suffers because he is not capable of showing and sharing his full humanness, a person who may be brought to experience joy.

There, where modern psychiatric science and our hearts meet, is the place in which help for the schizophrenic is to be found, and in which hopes for further goals are conceived, nourished, and activated.

* For a detailed illustration of this process, see S. Arieti, *Creativity: The Magic Synthesis* (New York: Basic Books, 1976).

Index

220 Index

MORE ABOUT PENGUINS, PELICANS AND PUFFINS

For further information about books available from Penguins please write to Dept EP, Penguin Books Ltd, Harmondsworth, Middlesex UB7 0DA.

In the U.S.A.: For a complete list of books available from Penguins in the United States write to Dept DG, Penguin Books, 299 Murray Hill Parkway, East Rutherford, New Jersey 07073.

In Canada: For a complete list of books available from Penguins in Canada write to Penguin Books Canada Ltd, 2801 John Street, Markham, Ontario L3R 1B4.

In Australia: For a complete list of books available from Penguins in Australia write to the Marketing Department, Penguin Books Australia Ltd, P.O. Box 257, Ringwood, Victoria 3134.

In New Zealand: For a complete list of books available from Penguins in New Zealand write to the Marketing Department, Penguin Books (N.Z.) Ltd, P.O. Box 4019, Auckland 10.

In India: For a complete list of books available from Penguins in India write to Penguin Overseas Ltd, 706 Eros Apartments, 56 Nehru Place, New Delhi 110019.